UNIX for Engineers

MW01250794

Scott D. James

Industrial & Manufacturing Systems Engineering
GMI Engineering and Management Institute

▲▲ **ADDISON-WESLEY**

An imprint of Addison Wesley Longman, Inc.

Menlo Park, California · Reading, Massachusetts · Harlow, England
Berkeley, California · Don Mills, Ontario · Sydney · Bonn · Amsterdam · Tokyo · Mexico City

UNIX for Engineers

AIX is a trademark, and IBM and OS/2 are registered trademarks of the International Business Machines Corporation

Apple, Mac, and Macintosh are registered trademarks of Apple Computer, Incorporated

AT&T, OpenLook, and System V are registered trademarks of AT&T

ANSI is a registered trademark of the American National Standards Institute

BSD is a trademark of the Regents of University of California at Berkeley

Hewlett Packard, HP, HP-UX, and HP LaserJet are trademarks of Hewlett Packard Company

Motif is a trademark of the Open System Foundation

MS-DOS, Microsoft, Microsoft Internet Explorer, Microsoft Windows, Microsoft Windows 95, and XENIX are registered trademarks of Microsoft Corporation

Netscape is a trademark of Netscape Communications

OpenLook, Solaris, SPARCstation, and SunOS are trademarks of Sun Microsystems, Incorporated

POSIX is a trademark of the Institute of Electronic and Electrical Engineers

SCO UNIX is a registered trademark of the Santa Cruz Operation

Star Trek: The Next Generation and Lt. Cmdr. Data are registered trademarks of Paramount Pictures

UNIX and X/Open are registered trademarks in the United States and other countries, licensed through X/Open Company Limited

X Windows is a trademark of the Massachusetts Institute of Technology

This is a module in the *Engineer's Toolkit*, an Addison-Wesley SELECT edition. Contact your sales representative for more information.

The Engineer's Toolkit is a trademark of Addison Wesley Longman, Inc.

Photo Credits:

Chapter 1: O2™ screen image of underwater camera courtesy of Katz Design, Inc., Montréal, Canada. O2™ workstation image courtesy of Silicon Graphics, Inc.

Chapter 2: courtesy of AT&T

Chapter 3: courtesy of NASA

Chapter 4: ©Archive Photos

Library of Congress catalog card number 95-131339.

ISBN: 0-8053-6488-9

1 2 3 4 5 6 7 8 9 10—CRK—01 00 99 98 97

Addison-Wesley Longman, Inc.
2725 Sand Hill Road
Menlo Park, CA 94025
http://www.aw.com/cseng/toolkit/

Contents

1

Introduction to the UNIX Operating System

Modern Computing Many great engineering achievements would not have been possible without the use of computers. Without the speed and power of UNIX workstations, for example, computer-aided design systems would still be in their infancy today. Computers have been used for engineering and scientific purposes since the 1950s and have now become virtually essential. This is due in part to the computer's ability to perform mundane tasks, which allows scientists and engineers to focus on the actual problem they are trying to solve. As computer sys-

tems have become faster and more powerful, the operating systems that allow users to work with the computer have had to mature as well. UNIX is one of the premier operating systems in use on computers today because of its power, capabilities, and portability—that is, the fact that it can operate on many different types of computers.

INTRODUCTION

This chapter provides a brief history of the UNIX operating system and discusses some of the different versions of UNIX that are available. It then introduces you to the basic components of a UNIX system. The chapter concludes with a warning about the use of the (CTRL) key in the UNIX environment and some other conventions used by UNIX and this book.

1-1 WHAT IS UNIX?

UNIX is one of the most widely used *operating systems* on computers today. The operating system is what allows the user to work with the computer. In addition to providing an interface for users, the operating system manages hardware components that may be connected to the computer, such as printers, disk drives, and monitors.

History

UNIX was written in the late 1960s at AT&T's Bell Laboratories in Murray Hill, New Jersey. The principal idea behind the design of UNIX was to make it very small and very fast. Making computers operate as fast as possible is always an important design consideration when creating an operating system. UNIX had to be small because of the limited amount of memory available on computers. At the time, the computer it was designed for had 8 K of memory; personal computers today come standard with around 16 MB (or 16,000 K) of memory.

UNIX was used internally at Bell Labs for quite some time, and it caught on quickly. The people who were primarily using UNIX were programmers and scientists, and UNIX was created with those folks in mind. It wasn't long before AT&T realized that UNIX had everything it needed to become a commercial operating system. UNIX had a distinct advantage over other operating systems available at the time: It could run on different types of computers. Many other operating systems that were available had been developed for a specific type of computer and could not run on any other type of system.

In 1974, Bell Labs licensed UNIX to universities for use in education. It was also made available to research labs. AT&T hoped to expand the use of UNIX and therefore create a commercial need for the operating system. AT&T's idea was simple: If college students learned and used UNIX at school, they would want to use UNIX on their jobs after college. One of the universities that received a copy was the University of California at Berkeley. This school added numerous enhancements to the original version of UNIX to make it more user friendly, programmer oriented, and interconnectable with other computers and devices. This branch of UNIX was called Berkeley Software Distribution, or BSD.

Once BSD was made available, the market for UNIX was opened. By the 1980s, many mainframes and minicomputers were offering UNIX as an operating system choice. Even Microsoft offered a PC-based version of UNIX called XENIX.

During the 1990s, the use of UNIX has continued to skyrocket. It is now one of the main operating systems in use. UNIX is available for just about every computer that is manufactured. High-end scientific and engineering applications are run on UNIX platforms, making the need to understand and use UNIX imperative for today's successful engineers.

Another aspect of UNIX that sets it apart from other operating systems is that it is a *multiuser* and *multitasking* operating system. Multiuser operating systems allow more than one user to work with the computer at a time. If you have worked on a PC or a Macintosh, you have experience with a single-user operating system. Multitasking operating systems allow multiple programs to be run simultaneously. The Microsoft MS-DOS operating system is a good example of a nonmultitasking operating system since it allows the user to run only one task at a time.

These two features—multiuser and multitasking capabilities—coupled with its portability to many different systems provide enormous power and flexibility to UNIX users.

Current Versions

Many different companies sell their own version of UNIX. The reason for this is that each company has added enhancements to the UNIX operating system that they feel make their version better than their competitors' versions. The following chart lists some of the various versions of UNIX that are available:

AIX	Advanced Interactive Executive: IBM's version of UNIX
BSD	Berkeley Software Distribution: University of California at Berkeley's UNIX variant
HP-UX	Hewlett-Packard's UNIX variant
Linux	A free PC-based version of UNIX
Sun OS	Sun Microsystems BSD-based version of UNIX
System V	The latest official release of AT&T UNIX (often referenced as SVR4—System V Release 4)
XENIX	A PC-based version of UNIX created by Microsoft and now developed by the Santa Cruz Operation (sometimes called SCO UNIX)

User Interfaces

Users interact with UNIX in two distinct ways: through the *command-line interface* and the *graphical user interface* (GUI). The command-line interface is simply a text-only screen interface in which the user types commands on a command line, and UNIX tries to execute those commands. The graphical user interface provides a look and feel similar to Microsoft Windows on a PC or the Macintosh computer's interface.

The most common UNIX graphical interface is called *X Windows*. X Windows was created at the Massachusetts Institute of Technology. Other vendors of UNIX have their own flavor of X Windows such as Sun Microsystems's OpenLook and HP's Motif. The reason for the different versions of the graphical user interface is that each vendor thinks its enhancements make it better than other graphical user interfaces that are available.

Future Trends

With so many choices of UNIX, where does the future of UNIX lie? The answer is in standardization. Currently, several different organizations are working on standardizing how UNIX works, looks, and feels. Some of these groups include the Institute of Electrical and Electronics Engineers (IEEE), which has created a standard for operating system portability, called Portable Operating Systems Standard for Computer Environments (POSIX). In Europe, a group known as X/Open is also working on standardization issues. This group has created the X/Open Portability Guide, which is similar to IEEE's POSIX. In the future, these two attempts at standardization will most likely merge into one common set of standards.

The future will also likely see UNIX systems that are increasingly faster, smaller, and cheaper. There are decent UNIX workstations that cost the same as high-end PCs. These workstations usually have more computing power and capabilities than the PC. Some people feel that as UNIX continues to be adopted into corporate America there may be a point where the UNIX workstation will replace the current desktop computer.

1-2 BASIC UNIX COMPONENTS

This section describes some of the basic components of a UNIX system.

The Filesystem

The *filesystem* is the mechanism that allows the information stored on a UNIX system to be managed in a logically structured, straightforward way. The filesystem consists primarily of two entities: *files* and *directories*. You can think of the filesystem as a kind of electronic file cabinet.

Files

Files are the most basic units of information that can be stored in the UNIX filesystem. Files can contain text, programs, data, images, sounds, or other items. Files are like the documents in a filing cabinet. For example, one file might contain your resume. Another file might contain the addresses of your friends, and so on. You can arrange these items so that they are kept separate to make them easy to retrieve and use.

Directories

If files are like the documents in a filing cabinet, then directories are like the drawers of a filing cabinet. It makes sense to keep similar documents clumped together. For example, you might keep all of your banking papers in one drawer in your file cabinet. You might keep school records, forms, and financial aid papers together in another drawer. Directories allow you to keep files together in the same way in your UNIX filesystem.

Directories in the UNIX filesystem are also known as hierarchical directories or trees. In other words, you can stick directories and files within directories, leading to a hierarchy. A directory that is contained in another directory is often called a subdirectory. The very top directory in the hierarchy is called the *root directory* and is denoted by the / character. All files and subdirectories must exist somewhere under the root in an upside-down treelike structure.

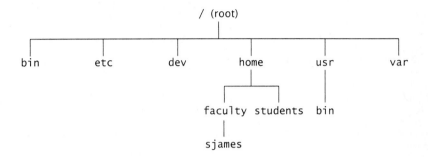

System Directories

As you explore your UNIX system, you will find that it includes many directories. The majority of these directories are system directories that contain files necessary for UNIX to be able to operate. In addition to the system directories, there are user directories in which UNIX users may store their own files. The following is a list of some directories that may be of particular interest to you:

/ This directory is called the root because it is the start of the directory *tree*. Every directory or file that exists on the computer must be somewhere under the root directory. The root directory also contains files for starting the computer.

/bin This directory contains many of the program files that are commonly needed by UNIX users. Programs to manage files and directories are stored in this directory.

/dev This directory contains all the system device files. If you look in the /dev directory, you will see many /dev/tty_ files, which are the UNIX computer's terminals. Files for the disk drives and serial ports also appear in this directory.

/etc This directory contains files that are used in system administration tasks. The *system administrator* is the person responsible for the maintenance of the UNIX computer system. Many of the files in this directory tell the UNIX computer about other computers it can communicate with. There are also files that explain how to print files and so forth.

/home (or something similar) This directory is where each individual user's *home directory* is stored. Many schools create more specific directories such as /faculty or /students for the same task. Users start out in their home directory when they login to the UNIX system. You should keep your personal files in your home directory. Each user can also specify whether other users have access to the files that are stored in his or her home directory.

/tmp This directory holds files that are needed only for a short time and then deleted. You can store files in /tmp, but note that this directory is cleared every time the computer system reboots.

/usr This directory stores most of the programs that are available to users.

/var This directory holds the system logging information, print jobs that are being sent to the printer, and incoming e-mail as it is being received.

Shells

The shell program provides the text interface for the user to communicate with the computer. The shell accepts commands from the user, interprets them, and then attempts to execute them. The most commonly used UNIX shell is the C shell, or **csh**. Many of the commands in this shell are based on the C programming language. It is worthwhile to mention that UNIX and C are very similar in grammatic structure. The reason is quite simple: C was developed to write UNIX. Therefore, you are hard pressed to find a UNIX version that does not include a C language compiler. By writing *shell scripts,* which are lists of commands that will be executed by the shell, you can use the shell as a simple programming language.

In addition to csh, many other shells containing different features are available, such as the Korn shell (*ksh*), the Turbo C shell (*tcsh*), the Bourne shell (which was the default AT&T shell), and the Bourne-again shell (*bash*). This module will present UNIX commands and features in a way that is independent of the shell used.

1-3   CONVENTIONS

This section describes some of the conventions that you need to know about when working with UNIX. A discussion of the (CTRL) key is presented, followed by UNIX conventions and conventions used in this book.

Control Characters

When working with UNIX, you will sometimes need to use a *control character* to perform a special task. To type a control character, you simply hold down the (CTRL) key while pressing some other key. Control characters are usually signified by the caret (^) symbol. For example, ^C means hold down (CTRL) and press C.

Some of the control characters have special functions in UNIX. Table 1-1 shows these keystrokes and their functions.

Table 1-1   Control Character Functions

Character	Function
^C	Interrupts (stops) the current activity
^D	Ends an open file; can also be used to logout
^H	Deletes the last character that was typed
^Q	Resumes paused screen output
^S	Pauses screen output
^U	Erases the command line
^W	Erases the last word
^Z	Suspends an executing job

Be very careful when typing to avoid accidentally pressing the (CTRL) key. As you proceed through this module, you will learn the appropriate uses of these control keys.

UNIX Conventions and This Book

UNIX is a case-sensitive operating system. You have to be very careful when typing commands into UNIX or they will not work. This book has been designed to reflect the proper use of UNIX commands and their respective case.

UNIX commands, and screen displays from the computer, will appear in this book in a monospaced, terminal-type font, like this: `ls`.

Files, directories, program names, and electronic addresses will appear italicized in the normal font, like this: *etc*.

Commands that are in a bold terminal-type font, such as `ls -l`, are actually typed into the UNIX computer. When you are trying examples in this book, be sure to press the Enter (or Return) key at the end of each command line. This key is usually labeled ⏎ on the keyboard.

SUMMARY

This chapter introduced you to some of the history and features of UNIX and to some of the basic components of a UNIX system. The chapter concluded with a short discussion of control characters and conventions. In the next chapter, you will learn about the essential UNIX commands you need to master to become an effective UNIX user.

Key Words

Command-line interface	Multiuser
Control character	Operating system
Directory	Root directory
File	Shell script
Filesystem	System administrator
Graphical user interface	Tree
Home directory	UNIX
Multitasking	X Windows

2 Fundamental UNIX Commands

Getting Started The commands that make up UNIX are very short in name yet powerful in capability. The command names had to be short to fit in the limited memory of the computer that UNIX was designed for. This reduction, to fit a given space, should remind you of the miniaturization of electronics. What used to take a full room of vacuum tubes was squeezed onto several boards of integrated circuits in the 1960s. The same UNIX commands running on those integrated circuit boards in the 1970s are today executed more quickly on a single microprocessor chip thanks to the advent of very large scale integration (VLSI) microprocessor technology.

INTRODUCTION

Whenever you want to work with a UNIX system, you must be familiar with a basic command set that will allow you to work with files and directories. If you have experience working with Microsoft DOS, many of the UNIX commands will seem familiar. If you are coming from a graphical user environment such as the Macintosh or Microsoft Windows, the idea of a command-line interface may seem somewhat cumbersome at first. Don't make the mistake of thinking that a text-based command-line interface is weak; in UNIX, extremely powerful tasks can be accomplished by writing just a command or two.

This chapter describes the basics of how to use the UNIX operating system. In this chapter, you will learn how to login and logout of your UNIX system. You will learn how to change and choose your password. You will learn how to navigate the directory tree and how to create and view text files. You will be introduced to file management and printing commands and to system security features. You will learn how to direct output to someplace other than the screen. You will also learn how to get help online.

2-1 ACCESSING YOUR UNIX ACCOUNT

The first tasks to master when working with UNIX are how to get into the system, how to get out of the system, and how to manage your password. This section will address these items.

Logging In to the System

UNIX systems, unlike personal computers, are on most of the time. Chances are your school has a minicomputer running UNIX that is located in an environmentally controlled room. To access the UNIX system, you have to login to it. The login process may take place on a dumb terminal, a PC, or a UNIX workstation.

In any event, before you are allowed access to the UNIX system, you must enter your username and your password at the login *prompt*. Your instructor, or someone from your school's computer department, may have to create an account for you on the UNIX system; you probably will not be able to do it yourself. If you are unsure how to get to the login prompt, you may want to ask one of these folks.

A typical login prompt screen might look like the following:

```
Linux 1.2.13 (zard.delpheus.com) (ttyp0)


zard login:
```

At this point, you are being asked to enter your username. Your *username* is usually some combination of your real name with the addition of some numbers. For example, my real name is Scott James, and my login name is sjames. Some schools will create a username such as jame1234, where the first four characters are the beginning of my last name, and the last four digits are from my student identification number. **One word of**

warning when working with UNIX: *Everything is case sensitive.* In other words sjames, SJAMES, and SJames are three different entities.

After you type your username and press the ⏎ key, you will be prompted for your password. You need to type the password and then press ⏎ again. You will notice that your password does not show up on the screen as you type it. This is a security feature to prevent other people from stealing your password.

If you didn't enter everything correctly, you will not be logged in to the system. The login prompt will reappear, and you will need to repeat the whole process. When you have successfully entered your username and password, you will see a screen that looks similar to the following. (From this point on, anything that is typed on the computer will appear in bold.)

```
Linux 1.2.13 (zard.delpheus.com) (ttyp0)


zard login: sjames
Password:
Last login: Mon Jul 1 22:45:04 on tty2
Linux 1.2.13.

You have new mail.
zard:~$
```

Notice that once you successfully enter your username and password, a command prompt appears. The command prompt is the last line in the preceding example. The command prompt usually includes the name of the computer that you are using (in this case, zard) and either a $ or % character to indicate where what you type will appear.

Logging Out of the System: logout

Getting on the system wasn't all that difficult. Getting out of the system is even easier. All you need to do is enter the logout command. You must press the ⏎ key after you type the command.

```
zard:~$ logout

Linux 1.2.13 (zard.delpheus.com) (ttyp0)


zard login:
```

Notice that the login prompt appears as soon as you have logged out. UNIX is now prepared for someone to login again. Some systems don't use the logout command; instead, they use the exit command. Most systems use one command or the other.

You should always make sure that you logout of the system when you are not using it. If you leave yourself logged in and walk away for even a minute, someone else can use your computer and send e-mail or messages using your user identity, or destroy your work and files.

Changing Your Password: passwd

When you want to change your password, you use the `passwd` command. To use this command, you must know the old password. This requirement prevents people from randomly changing anyone else's password.

You should change your password at least once if the original password you were given was created by someone else. Many schools use a fairly simple scheme to generate initial passwords for computer accounts. If someone figures out this scheme and you haven't changed your password from the original one, your password could be changed or used by someone else.

Here is an example of the `passwd` command. Note that the ⏎ key must be pressed after the command is typed.

```
zard:~$ passwd

Changing password for sjames
Enter old password:
Enter new password:
Re-type new password:
Password changed.

zard:~$
```

Note that after you enter your old password, you are asked to enter your new password twice. This is to ensure that you correctly typed the password the way that you want it. If you don't enter the old password correctly or don't type the new password the same way both times, you would see the following error message: `Password not changed`.

When you are trying to choose a password, here are some rules to follow to help make it a good one.

- Don't use the names of family members or friends.
- Don't use other information about yourself that can be easily guessed, such as your birth date.
- Don't use words that can be looked up in a dictionary, even foreign words, since there are password-cracking programs that use dictionaries.
- Make the password at least six characters long.
- Use both uppercase and lowercase letters if possible.
- Throw in a number or two.
- Put in a special punctuation character such as !, @, #, $, %, ^, or &.
- Don't give your password to anyone for any reason. If a person logs in as you, that person effectively becomes you and can do anything you can do: send e-mail, delete files, and so on.

With all these rules, how do you pick a good password that's easily remembered? One way is to choose a line from a poem or song and use the first letter of each word: "London Bridge is falling down" becomes Lbifd. If you throw in a special character at the beginning and some numbers at the end, you get !Lbifd96. This is a secure password that's easily remembered and conforms to the rules stated here.

Try It In this Try It!, you'll login to your UNIX account, change your password, and logout of the system.

1. Login to your UNIX account at the login prompt by typing your username followed by ↵. Wait until prompted for your password, and then type your password followed by ↵. Make sure that you are logged on; you should see a command prompt if you were successful. If you weren't successful, try logging in again.

2. Type the command **passwd** ↵. You will be prompted for your old (current) password. Type what you want the new password to be and press ↵ again. The computer will then ask you to confirm your new password. Retype it and press ↵ again. If you were successful, you should see the message Password changed.

3. Logout of the system by typing the command **logout** (or **exit**) followed by ↵.

4. Try to login again with your new password.

2-2 NAVIGATING THE DIRECTORY TREE

This section examines how to move around the directory tree. You will learn how to find out what is in a directory, how to move from directory to directory, and how to create and remove directories.

Listing a Directory's Contents: ls

When you want to see what is in a *directory,* you use the ls command. (From this point forward, it is assumed that the ↵ key will be pressed after each command.) Remember from Chapter 1 that directories can contain subdirectories and files. Let's see what is in my *home directory.*

```
zard:~$ ls
Mail/     a.out*     povray/    testit.c  xball/
zard:~$
```

Five items are listed. You can tell that three of the five are directories: *Mail, povray,* and *xball.* You know these are directories because each of the names is followed by a / character. The other two items, *a.out* and *testit.c,* are *files. a.out* is not just a normal file; it is a program file that I can run. An asterisk (*) after a filename indicates a program file, or more precisely, an *executable file.*

The basic ls command provides a quick look at what is in the current directory. You can also tell UNIX to look in a specific directory by specifying the directory name after the command. For example, if you wanted to see what is in the *povray* directory, you would enter the following:

```
zard:~$ ls povray
POVBIN_0.GZ    POVDOC_2.GZ    POVRAY_2.REA   POVSRC_0.GZ
POVBIN_1.GZ    POVINC_2.GZ    POVSCN_2.GZ    POVSRC_1.GZ
zard:~$
```

From this output, you can see that there are eight normal files (no / or * after the filenames) in the *povray* directory.

Not all versions of the UNIX ls command automatically provide the program and directory markings. If your version doesn't, try the command ls -F. You can see from the following example that ls and ls -F do the same thing on my UNIX system.

```
zard:~$ ls -F
Mail/    a.out*    povray/    testit.c xball/
zard:~$ ls -F povray
POVBIN_0.GZ    POVDOC_2.GZ    POVRAY_2.REA    POVSRC_0.GZ
POVBIN_1.GZ    POVINC_2.GZ    POVSCN_2.GZ     POVSRC_1.GZ
zard:~$
```

If you want to get more information about each entity in a subdirectory, try the ls -l command. This version of ls will produce a long listing, that shows the file type, the permissions of the file or directory, the link count, the owner of the file or directory, the group the file or directory belongs to, the size of the file or directory, the date the file or directory was created or last modified, and the file or directory name. The link count (second column) tells how many links, or pointers, to a particular file or directory there are on the system. Links are sometimes created as shortcuts or nicknames to a file or directory.

```
zard:~$ ls -l
total 8
drwx------    2 sjames    users         1024 Jun 20 13:10 Mail/
-rwxr-xr-x    1 sjames    users         3933 Jun 23 09:29 a.out*
drwxr-xr-x    2 sjames    users         1024 Jul  2 02:30 povray/
-rw-r--r--    1 sjames    users           70 Jun 23 09:29 testit.c
drwxr-xr-x    2 sjames    users         1024 Jun 27 11:21 xball/
zard:~$
```

If you study the output, you can see that *Mail, povray,* and *xball* all have a d in the first column, indicating that they are directories. (The other letters in this column indicate rights and permissions; you'll learn about these in Section 2-7.) You can also see that *sjames* owns all the items. The group *users* has access to the items if *sjames* has given them access. You can also see the size, creation date and time, and name of each file or directory.

ls -a is another important version of the ls command. The -a tells UNIX to show all files, including hidden files. Any file or directory in UNIX that starts with a period (.) is a hidden file. Hidden files are usually used for program setup and shell configuration information. Since most users are not interested in these files, they are normally hidden from ls output. Let's see what ls -a turns up.

```
zard:~$ ls -a
./               .elm/           .lessrc        a.out*       xball/
../              .kermrc         .term/         povray/
.bash_history    .less           Mail/          testit.c
zard:~$
```

As you can see, there were quite a few hidden directories and files. Let's look at two of them. The . directory refers to the current directory, and the .. directory refers to the parent directory; both names are convenient shorthand you can use when working with the directory tree. Suppose you want to see a long listing of what was in the parent directory of your home directory. Further, you want to see all the files and directories that are stored there. UNIX will allow you to do this all in one command: ls -al .. . Remember that the -al tells the system to display all files in long-listing format. The .. signifies the parent directory of the directory that you are currently in. Here's the output of that command for my current directory.

```
zard:~$ ls -al ..
total 17
drwxr-xr-x   6 root      root          1024 Jun 20 13:08 ./
drwxr-xr-x  17 root      root          1024 Aug  7  1995 ../
drwxrwxr-x   8 root      wheel         1024 Jun 20 08:11 ftp/
drwxr-xr-x   2 root      root         12288 Jun 20 06:53 lost+found/
drwxr-xr-x   7 sjames    users         1024 Jul  2 02:30 sjames/
drwxr-xr-x   5 vjames    users         1024 Jun 20 13:12 vjames/
zard:~$
```

Printing the Current (Working) Directory: pwd

Now you can see what's in a directory, but how can you tell what directory you are in? The pwd command shows you.

```
zard:~$ pwd
/home/sjames
zard:~$
```

I have to confess that the command line has actually been telling me what directory I've been in the whole time. UNIX provides another short-cut for its users: The ~ (tilde) character means home directory; in my case, ~ is equal to */home/sjames*. If you look at the command prompt line in the examples shown so far, you will see a ~ to indicate the home directory.

Many UNIX system administrators set up the system so that the command prompt displays the current directory. If this is not the case for your system, simply use the pwd command to figure out where you are.

Changing Directories: cd

If you want to move from your home directory to somewhere else, you need to use the cd command. cd stands for change directory. If I want to go to my system's root directory and have a look around, I would enter the following:

```
zard:~$ cd /
zard:/$ ls
bin/     dev/       lib/          proc/     tmp/      vmlinuz
boot/    etc/       lost+found/   root/     usr/
cdrom/   home/      mnt/          sbin/     var/
zard:/$
```

Notice that the command prompt properly displays the / to signify that I am at the root directory. If I quickly want to get back to my home directory, I can type **cd ~** to do that.

```
zard:~$ cd ~
zard:~$ ls
Mail/    a.out*    povray/   testit.c xball/
zard:~$
```

On most UNIX systems, typing **cd** is the same thing as typing **cd ~**.

Absolute Pathing Versus Relative Pathing

You can move around the UNIX directory tree in two ways. You can specify the location with regard to the root directory. This is known as *absolute pathing* and always starts with the / character, therefore telling UNIX how to get to the destination subdirectory from the root directory. The second way is to use *relative pathing*, in which you use the .. (parent) directory notation to specify that you want to move relative to your current location.

For example, suppose I want to get into my *povray* directory. I issue the command **cd povray**. I look around and decide that I want to go back up one directory, to my home directory. How can I do it? Using absolute referencing, I would enter **cd /home/sjames**. Let's try it and see the results.

```
zard:~$ cd povray
zard:~/povray$ ls
POVBIN_0.GZ    POVDOC_2.GZ    POVRAY_2.REA   POVSRC_0.GZ
POVBIN_1.GZ    POVINC_2.GZ    POVSCN_2.GZ    POVSRC_1.GZ
zard:~/povray$ cd /home/sjames
zard:~$ ls
Mail/    a.out*    povray/   testit.c xball/
zard:~$
```

It works! I could accomplish the same thing, though, by simply saying that I need to move up one directory from where I am currently, that is, by telling UNIX to go to the parent directory of this directory via the cd .. command.

```
zard:~$ cd povray
zard:~/povray$ ls
POVBIN_0.GZ    POVDOC_2.GZ    POVRAY_2.REA   POVSRC_0.GZ
POVBIN_1.GZ    POVINC_2.GZ    POVSCN_2.GZ    POVSRC_1.GZ
zard:~/povray$ cd ..
zard:~$ ls
Mail/    a.out*    povray/   testit.c xball/
zard:~$
```

I got the same result. I also could have typed **cd ~** which is the shortcut to my home directory. Let's go to the root and then quickly get to my *povray* directory.

```
zard:~$ cd /
zard:/$ ls
bin/      dev/          lib/          proc/       tmp/           vmlinuz
boot/     etc/          lost+found/   root/       usr/
cdrom/    home/         mnt/          sbin/       var/
zard:/$ cd ~/povray
zard:~/povray$ ls
POVBIN_0.GZ    POVDOC_2.GZ    POVRAY_2.REA   POVSRC_0.GZ
POVBIN_1.GZ    POVINC_2.GZ    POVSCN_2.GZ    POVSRC_1.GZ
zard:~/povray$
```

Which is better to use: relative or absolute pathing? The answer is nei-
ther; you will need to be able to use both. Relative pathing is very handy if
you want to move up a little bit or if you are in the middle of a really long
path. Absolute pathing is nice if you know exactly where something is
located off the root directory.

Using Wildcard Characters

Sometimes a directory will include so many files and subdirectories that
you can't see them all on one screen. If you know part of the name of the
entity that you are looking for, you can use a *wildcard character* to help
you locate it. For example, let's switch to the */etc* directory and look
around. If you perform an ls command, you will usually see about a page
and a half of files and directories. What can you do if you want to find
files that start with the letter *n*? The answer is to use a wildcard character.

Three different wildcard characters are available in UNIX. The first character is the *, which is used to match any number of characters. The second wildcard character is the ?, which is used to match a single character.
The third wildcard character is the [ ], which is used to match any character that is enclosed inside the brackets. Let's examine how each works.

If I want to find all the entities in my */etc* directory starting with the letter *n*, I can type the following:

```
zard:/etc$ cd /etc
zard:/etc$ ls n*
named.boot  networks    nntpserver
zard:/etc$
```

You can see that any file that starts with the letter *n* is shown, regard-
less of how long the filename is.

The ? wildcard character is useful when you want to match a given
number of characters. For example, to find any filename that starts with
the letter *n* and has a *t* as the third letter in its name, I can enter

```
zard:/etc$ ls n?t*
networks    nntpserver
zard:/etc$
```

You can see that *networks* and *nntpserver* are both selected because
they each start with the letter *n* and have a *t* as the third letter.

The third wildcard character is the [ ] set. Whatever is placed in the brackets will be matched. For example, to find all entities that start with an *a*, *c*, or *n*, I can enter

```
zard:/etc$ ls [acn]*
at.deny   csh.cshrc  csh.login  named.boot  networks  nntpserver
zard:/etc$
```

Wildcard characters can be mixed and matched and are extremely powerful tools when used with the ls command to help locate files and directories.

Making Directories: mkdir

To create, or make, a directory, you use the mkdir command. For example, suppose I want to create a directory called *scott1*. I will first make sure that I am in my home directory ~. I will then create the directory, use ls to ensure that it exists, and then change to it.

```
zard:~/etc$ cd ~
zard:~$ mkdir scott1
zard:~$ ls
Mail/     a.out*     povray/    scott1/    testit.c  xball/
zard:~$ cd scott1
```

It is also possible to create more than one directory at a time. Let's create three subdirectories under the *scott1* directory, starting from the ~ directory.

```
zard:~/scott1$ cd ~
zard:~$ mkdir scott1/dir1 scott1/dir2 scott1/dir3
zard:~$ cd scott1
zard:~/scott1$ ls -l
total 3
drwxr-xr-x   2 sjames   users        1024 Jul  2 03:36 dir1/
drwxr-xr-x   2 sjames   users        1024 Jul  2 03:36 dir2/
drwxr-xr-x   2 sjames   users        1024 Jul  2 03:36 dir3/
zard:~/scott1$
```

We could have just as easily created the three subdirectories while we were in the *scott1* directory by typing **mkdir dir1 dir2 dir3**.

Naming Files and Directories in UNIX

When you are creating files and directories, you can name them pretty much anything that you want. You are best off using only letters, numbers, periods (.), and underscores (_). These characters are guaranteed to keep you out of trouble. Remember that UNIX is case sensitive, and thus lowercase and uppercase letters are not the same thing.

The following list of characters should be avoided when naming files or directories:

```
  !     @     #     $     &     ^     ()     {}      '      "
  *     ;     ?     |     /     \     <>     ~       ,   (SPACE) (TAB)
```

Although UNIX may let you use some of these characters in a file or directory name, you may not be able to access the file or directory after you create it. Note that the slash (/) used to indicate a directory is not actually part of the filename.

Removing Directories: `rmdir`

The `rmdir` command is used to remove existing empty directories. Like `mkdir`, you can remove multiple directories with one `rmdir` command. If the directory to be removed is not empty, the error message `Directory not empty` will appear, as you see here.

```
zard:~/scott1$ cd ~
zard:~$ rmdir scott1
rmdir: scott1: Directory not empty
zard:~$ cd scott1
zard:~/scott1$ ls
dir1/  dir2/  dir3/
zard:~/scott1$ rmdir dir1 dir2
zard:~/scott1$ ls
dir3/
zard:~/scott1$ cd ..
zard:~$ rmdir scott1
rmdir: scott1: Directory not empty
zard:~$
```

When I tried to remove the *scott1* directory, I got an error message since the three subdirectories that I created underneath it were still there. I then changed into the *scott1* directory and removed *dir1* and *dir2*. I then went back up one directory and tried to remove the *scott1* directory again. I still got the error message `Directory not empty` since the *dir3* subdirectory is still located in *scott1*.

I can finish deleting the *scott1* directory by removing it and the *dir3* subdirectory all on the same line. I will then perform the `ls` command, and things should be back to the way they were when we started this section.

```
zard:~$ rmdir scott1/dir3 scott1
zard:~$ ls
Mail/    a.out*    povray/    testit.c xball/
zard:~$
```

Try It   This Try It! lets you practice using the `ls` and subdirectory commands.

1. Find the absolute path to your home directory by typing
   pwd ⏎

2. Change to the root directory and take a look around by typing
   cd / ⏎
   ls ⏎

3. Change back to your home directory and create a subdirectory called *test*.
   cd ~ ⏎
   mkdir test ⏎

4. Change to the *test* directory and create another subdirectory called *test2*. Make sure that *test2* exists:

```
cd test ⏎
mkdir test2 ⏎
ls -aF test2 ⏎
```

5. Go back up one directory and try to remove *test*. You should get an error message. Try removing *test2* first; then remove *test*.

```
cd .. ⏎
rmdir test ⏎
rmdir test/test2 ⏎
rmdir test ⏎
```

6. Confirm that *test* is gone.

```
ls -aF ⏎
```

2-3 A QUICK INTRODUCTION TO THE *vi* TEXT EDITOR

This section provides a quick overview of how to create text files with the vi *text editor*. Although not a particularly nice text editor to use, every UNIX system includes *vi* as a standard text editor, and many applications use *vi* as the default text editor. Therefore, it is important that you learn how to maneuver around in *vi.*

vi Basics

vi is a full-screen text editor that is somewhat crude by today's standards. What you see on the screen is exactly what will be written out to a file when you tell *vi* to do so. To start *vi,* you type **vi** or **vi *filename*.** If *vi* is editing a new file, the text [New File] will appear on the very bottom line of the screen. If a filename was provided when *vi* was started, that name will appear in double quotation marks on the last line as well.

    vi operates in three different modes.

- *Command mode* is used for screen navigation, deletion, and pasting operations.
- *Input mode* is used to insert, change, or update text.
- *Last-line mode* is used for global operations such as saving files and performing searches.

When *vi* is started, it is automatically placed in the command mode. To begin writing text, you press a (append) or i (insert) to switch to input mode. Make sure that you are using lowercase command letters since *vi* is case sensitive. Be sure to press the ⏎ key at the end of each line. If you want to change from input mode to command mode, press the (ESC) key. To change from input mode to last-line mode, press (ESC) followed by a :, /, or ?. You may also press the (ESC) key anytime you don't remember which mode you are in to return to the command mode.

    Let's create a new file in *vi* called *firstfile.*

```
zard:~$ vi firstfile
~
~
~
~
~
~
~
~
~
~
~
~
~
~
~
~
~
~
~
~
~
~
 "firstfile" [NEW FILE]  1 line, 1 char
```

(I've shown the full screen in this first representation of the *vi* working environment. In the screens that follow, redundant, non-essential screen data is replaced with an ellipsis [⋮].)

You see that *firstfile* is a new file as indicated by the last line. You can then press i to enter insert mode so that you can start typing.

```
This is the first file that I have typed in vi.
vi isn't all that difficult to use...
    it just takes practice.
~
```

$$[\,\vdots\,]$$

```
~
```

You can make corrections by using the (BKSP) key when you are in input mode. Then press (ESC) to return to command mode.

Suppose that you now want to save this file. To save your file to disk, you have to enter last-line mode, which is done by pressing the :, /, or ? key. Once the : shows up on the last line, you need to enter a command from the following set:

w   Writes the file
w!   Overwrites any existing file with the same name
q!   Quits vi and loses any changes
wq!   Overwrites any existing file and then quits *vi*

Let's save the file and get out of *vi* by entering **:wq!**

```
vi isn't all that difficult to use...
    it just takes practice.
~
```

$$[\,\vdots\,]$$

```
~
:wq!
```

Then use `ls` to take a peek after executing the command. The file *firstfile* appears in the list.

```
zard:~$ ls -l
total 9
drwx------   2 sjames   users       1024 Jun 20 13:10 Mail/
-rwxr-xr-x   1 sjames   users       3933 Jun 23 09:29 a.out*
-rw-r--r--   1 sjames   users        114 Jul  2 04:25 firstfile
drwxr-xr-x   2 sjames   users       1024 Jul  2 02:30 povray/
-rw-r--r--   1 sjames   users         70 Jun 23 09:29 testit.c
drwxr-xr-x   2 sjames   users       1024 Jun 27 11:21 xball/
zard:~$
```

Moving Around in *vi*

The (BKSP) key will allow you to make corrections only to the line that you are currently working with in the input mode. How can you move around to other parts of a long file and make corrections? Table 2-1 lists the screen navigation keys. Note that you must be in command mode to use these keys.

Table 2-1   Screen Navigation Keys in the vi Editor

Keystroke(s)	Movement
(→) or l	Moves one character right
(←) or h	Moves one character left
(↓) or j	Moves down one line
(↑) or k	Moves up one line
(CTRL)-d	Scrolls down one-half screen
(CTRL)-u	Scrolls up one-half screen
(CTRL)-f	Scrolls forward one page
(CTRL)-b	Scrolls backward one page
0	Moves to the start of a line
$	Moves to the end of a line
w	Moves right one word
b	Moves left one word

Some of these navigation commands can be preceded by a number for a more powerful operation. For example, 25j will move down the file 25 lines, and 5w will move forward 5 words.

Inserting Text

Many times you will use *vi* with files that already contain information. Here's how you add text to a file. First position your cursor at the location where you want to insert new text, and make sure you are in command mode, then press one of the following keys:

a   Appends text after the cursor
A   Appends text at the end of the line
o   Opens a line below the line the cursor is on and places the cursor
         at the first column of the new line
O   Opens a line above the line the cursor is on and places the cursor
         at the first column of the new line
i   Inserts text before the cursor
I   Inserts text at the beginning of the line

Deleting Text

You can delete text in command mode by pressing the following keys:

x   Deletes a character
dw   Deletes a word
dd   Deletes a line
d0   Deletes to the beginning of the line
d$ Deletes to the end of the line
dG   Deletes to the end of the file

This section hasn't covered everything that can be done in *vi*, but you should now have a solid foundation for working with *vi*. Most UNIX systems provide a much nicer text editor. Appendix A will briefly discuss some of these other text editors and provide more details on advanced operations with *vi*.

Try It

The only way that you will get good at *vi* is to practice using it. This Try It! will assist you in performing some of the basic operations.

1. Run *vi* and enter a new filename, for example, vi testit ⏎.

2. The screen should clear, and [New File] should now be displayed at the bottom of the file. You are automatically put in command mode after you open a file, so press i to enter input mode to start inserting text.

3. Type three or four lines. Make sure you press the ⏎ key at the end of each line.

4. Practice moving around and deleting information. Remember you have to be in command mode, so press the (ESC) key to switch from input mode to command mode. Refer to the previous pages for the keystrokes that can be used to move around in *vi* and how to delete text.

5. Try moving to different locations to see what the differences are appending (the a operations), opening (the o operations), and inserting (the i operations). Remember that each of these operations will put you in input mode, and you must press the (ESC) key to return to command mode.

6. When you are finished experimenting with *vi*, make sure you have a few lines left in your file. To save your file, switch to the last-line mode by pressing (ESC). Then type **wq!** to write your file to disk and quit *vi*.

2-4 VIEWING FILES

In the last section, you learned how to use the *vi* editor to create or modify text files. This section will show you how you can simply look at files without actually opening them up in a text editor.

I have created the following file called *viewfile,* which is 30 lines long. I also numbered every fifth line so that you can see the effects of the various file-viewing commands. We will be looking at the contents of this file in this section, so here is a copy of the entire file.

```
I created this file.
There are a total of thirty lines in it.
UNIX isn't so hard to learn;
it just takes a little time
5 - and a little effort on
your part, but soon you will
see that it will pay off.
If you want to become good at
using UNIX, you have to practice.
10 - At first it may be a little cumbersome,
but it won't take
too long before
all of those
short commands
15 - will seem second nature.
Another great part
of using UNIX is
all of the incredible
applications that have
20 - been written for it.
Many scientific and engineering
applications exist only on UNIX
workstations; there simply
are no equivalents on
25 - personal computer platforms.
If you are serious about
computers, you should get
serious about learning,
exploring, and using
30 - UNIX.
```

Viewing the Entire File at Once: cat

The first command you might use to view a file is called cat. A useful tool for looking at short files, cat has a problem when looking at larger files—long files tend to scroll on by, and you end up being able to read only the last screenful of the file. For example, if you enter the command **cat viewfile**, you will not be able to see the first few lines because they will have scrolled off the top of the screen.

```
If you want to become good at
using UNIX, you have to practice.
10 - At first it may be a little cumbersome,
but it won't take
too long before
all of those
short commands
15 - will seem second nature.
Another great part
```

```
of using UNIX is
all of the incredible
applications that have
20 - been written for it.
Many scientific and engineering
applications exist only on UNIX
workstations; there simply
are no equivalents on
25 - personal computer platforms.
If you are serious about
computers, you should get
serious about learning,
exploring, and using
30 - UNIX.

zard:~$
```

Here's where some of those control characters mentioned in Chapter 1 can come in handy. If you realize that the file is really long and you want to try to pause it yourself, you can press (CTRL)-**S** to stop the screen from scrolling. To resume the scrolling action again, press the (CTRL)-**Q** key combination. If you decide you don't want to see the remainder of the file at any point, press the (CTRL)-**C** combination to interrupt the `cat` command.

Keep in mind that files that are only two or three screens in length will be displayed by `cat` so quickly that the (CTRL) commands probably won't be able to pause them. You can, however, pause these files by using the `more` command.

Viewing Text a Screenful at a Time: `more`

One way to overcome the problem of the file scrolling is to use the `more` command. `more` will allow you to see the contents of a file one screenful at a time. For example, you can type the `more viewfile` command to see the first screenful of the file.

```
zard:~$ more viewfile
I created this file.
There are a total of thirty lines in it.
UNIX isn't so hard to learn;
it just takes a little time
5 - and a little effort on
your part, but soon you will
see that it will pay off.
If you want to become good at
using UNIX, you have to practice.
10 - At first it may be a little cumbersome,
but it won't take
too long before
all of those
short commands
15 - will seem second nature.
Another great part
of using UNIX is
all of the incredible
applications that have
20 - been written for it.
Many scientific and engineering
applications exist only on UNIX
--More--(75%)
```

The --More-- prompt on the last line reminds you that there is more of the file left to view. The 75% indicates that you have seen 75 percent of the entire file. At the --More-- prompt, there are four keys that you can press.

q   Quits more and returns to the UNIX prompt
b   Goes back one page in the file
⏎   Displays the next line in the file
(SPACE) Goes to the next page in the file

Another powerful feature of the more command is the ability to search for text that you specify. At the --More-- prompt, if you press the / key followed by the text you want more to search for and the ⏎ key, more will attempt to find the input text. If more cannot find the text that you asked it to look for, you will receive the message Pattern Not Found; otherwise, more will skip forward and display the text that you asked it to find.

Viewing Partial Files: head and tail

Sometimes you don't want to view a whole file, perhaps you are interested in seeing only the first few lines or the last few lines. The commands head and tail, respectively, perform these tasks.

```
zard:~$ head viewfile
I created this file.
There are a total of thirty lines in it.
UNIX isn't so hard to learn;
it just takes a little time
5 - and a little effort on
your part, but soon you will
see that it will pay off.
If you want to become good at
using UNIX, you have to practice.
10 - At first it may be a little cumbersome,
```

As you can see, the head command shows the first ten lines of the file. The tail command shows the last ten lines of the file.

```
zard:~$ tail viewfile
applications exist only on UNIX
workstations; there simply
are no equivalents on
25 - personal computer platforms.
If you are serious about
computers, you should get
serious about learning,
exploring, and using
30 - UNIX.

zard:~$
```

2-5 FILE MANAGEMENT COMMANDS

This section examines commands that deal with the maintenance of files within the UNIX filesystem: the commands for copying, renaming, moving, and removing files.

Copying Files: cp

You will often need to copy files. UNIX provides the cp command to carry out this task. cp requires two pieces of information before it can perform its work: the location of the source (original) files or directories that you want copied and the destination for the files or directories. The cp command has the following syntax: cp *sourcedir/file destinationdir/file*.

Let's create a second directory *povray2* and then copy all the files from *povray* into *povray2*.

```
zard:~$ cd ~
zard:~$ mkdir povray2
zard:~$ cd povray
zard:~/povray$ cp * ../povray2
zard:~/povray$ cd ../povray2
zard:~/povray2$ ls
POVBIN_0.GZ    POVDOC_2.GZ    POVRAY_2.REA    POVSRC_0.GZ
POVBIN_1.GZ    POVINC_2.GZ    POVSCN_2.GZ     POVSRC_1.GZ
zard:~/povray2$
```

You can see from the ls command that the copy was successful. If you take a closer look at the cp command itself, you can see that I told it to copy *, which means all files, into a directory called *povray2,* located just under the parent of *povray* (..). As you get more proficient at UNIX, you will find yourself using wildcard characters and relative addressing often.

You could have achieved the same results by entering either of the following two sets of commands:

```
zard:~$ cd ~
zard:~$ mkdir povray2
zard:~$ cp povray/* povray2
```

```
zard:~$ cd ~
zard:~$ mkdir povray2
zard:~$ cp povray povray2
```

cp is not a very bright command in that it will overwrite any file that has the same name as a file that it is attempting to copy. To make cp a little bit smarter, you can use the -i switch, which makes cp ask whether or not you want it to overwrite an existing file. For example, if I now copy the contents of *povray* to *povray2* with the -i switch active, I am asked whether the files should be overwritten.

```
zard:~$ cp -i povray/* povray2
cp: overwrite `povray2/POVBIN_0.GZ'?
```

If I enter **n**, cp will stop; if I enter **y**, cp will overwrite the existing file.

Renaming or Moving Files: mv

mv is one of the UNIX commands with multiple purposes. You can use mv to move files or directories from one directory location to another location. You can also use mv to rename files or directories. How can you tell which operation is going to take place? If there is no destination component of the mv command, the command will perform a rename operation. If the destination does exist, a move operation will be performed. The mv command has the following syntax: mv *sourcedir/file destinationdir/file*.

Let's look first at renaming. Suppose I want to rename *viewfile* to *junkfile*, and to rename the directory *povray2* to *render*.

```
zard:~$ mv viewfile junkfile
zard:~$ mv povray2 render
zard:~$ ls -l
total 11
drwx------   2 sjames   users       1024 Jun 20 13:10 Mail/
-rwxr-xr-x   1 sjames   users       3933 Jun 23 09:29 a.out*
-rw-r--r--   1 sjames   users        114 Jul  2 04:25 firstfile
-rw-r--r--   1 sjames   users        758 Jul  5 11:40 junkfile
drwxr-xr-x   2 sjames   users       1024 Jul  2 02:30 povray/
drwxr-xr-x   2 sjames   users       1024 Jul  5 12:17 render/
-rw-r--r--   1 sjames   users         70 Jun 23 09:29 testit.c
drwxr-xr-x   2 sjames   users       1024 Jun 27 11:21 xball/
zard:~$
```

You can see from the output of the ls command that the file *viewfile* was renamed *junkfile* and that the directory *povray2* became *render*.

Now let's examine how to move files. Let's say that I want to tidy up my home directory by creating a subdirectory called *scottstuff*. I then want to move all of my files with filenames that end in *file* into *scottstuff*.

```
zard:~$ mkdir scottstuff
zard:~$ mv *file scottstuff
zard:~$ ls -l
total 10
drwx------   2 sjames   users       1024 Jun 20 13:10 Mail/
-rwxr-xr-x   1 sjames   users       3933 Jun 23 09:29 a.out*
drwxr-xr-x   2 sjames   users       1024 Jul  2 02:30 povray/
drwxr-xr-x   2 sjames   users       1024 Jul  5 12:17 render/
drwxr-xr-x   2 sjames   users       1024 Jul  5 12:33 scottstuff/
-rw-r--r--   1 sjames   users         70 Jun 23 09:29 testit.c
drwxr-xr-x   2 sjames   users       1024 Jun 27 11:21 xball/
zard:~$
```

You can see from the output of the ls command that both *firstfile* and *junkfile* were moved into *scottstuff*. I can enter another ls command to confirm this:

```
zard:~$ cd scottstuff/
zard:~/scottstuff$ ls -l
total 2
-rw-r--r--   1 sjames   users        114 Jul  2 04:25 firstfile
-rw-r--r--   1 sjames   users        758 Jul  5 11:40 junkfile
zard:~/scottstuff$
```

Removing Files: rm

To delete or remove files, you use the rm command. If you want to remove a single file, or multiple files, you just put the filenames after the rm command. Let's say that I want to get rid of the two files that I placed in the *scottstuff* directory. I can get rid of them by typing the following rm command.

```
zard:~/scottstuff$ ls -l
total 2
-rw-r--r--    1 sjames    users         114 Jul  2 04:25 firstfile
-rw-r--r--    1 sjames    users         758 Jul  5 11:40 junkfile
zard:~/scottstuff$ rm firstfile junkfile
zard:~/scottstuff$ ls -l
total 0
zard:~/scottstuff$
```

Watch out! UNIX is not like the Macintosh, MS-DOS, or Windows 95—once you delete a file or directory, it is gone. There is no undelete command; the best that you can hope for is to get whatever might have been backed up by your school's computer center when the last backup was performed on your account. Fortunately, most schools back up files every night. Another good idea to minimize lost work is to create backup copies of any important files you may have by using the cp command.

Try It This Try It! lets you practice the file management skills in this section by creating three files in *vi* and then moving them around.

1. Create three files in *vi* (they can contain whatever text you like).

    cd ~ ⏎
    vi myfile1 ⏎
    vi myfile2 ⏎
    vi myfile3 ⏎

2. Make a new directory for the files called *filedir*.

    mkdir filedir ⏎

3. Copy the files into the *filedir* directory.

    cp myfile? filedir ⏎

4. Make sure that the files are in the directory.

    ls -l filedir ⏎

5. Delete the *myfile2* file in the *filedir* directory.

    rm filedir/myfile2 ⏎

6. Move the original *myfile2* file into the *filedir* directory.

    mv myfile2 filedir ⏎

7. Delete the remaining two *myfile* files in your home directory.

    rm myfile? ⏎

8. Change to the *filedir* directory and make sure you have all three files.

    cd filedir ⏎
    ls -l ⏎

9. Rename *myfile3* to *thirdfile*.

    `mv myfile3 thirdfile`⏎

10. Enter the `ls` command to make sure that the renaming worked.

    `ls -l`⏎

2-6 PRINTING FILES AND PRINT QUEUE MANAGEMENT

Files that you type are only so useful if you can't print them. This section will discuss how to print files and how to manage the items that you send to be printed.

Printing Files: lpr

The `lpr` command sends files to the printer that you specify on the command line. To effectively use the `lpr` command, you may have to talk to your instructor or computer center to learn the names of the printers that you have the ability to print to.

If you want to keep other UNIX users happy, make sure that you send text files to text file printers. If you are curious whether or not something is a plain text file, use one of the viewing commands discussed in Section 2-4. If you can read the contents of the file, the printer should be able to print it.

Let's take a look at several different examples of using the `lpr` command.

The following command prints a file using the most basic `lpr` syntax:

`lpr myfile`⏎

This example would attempt to print the file called *myfile* to the default printer hooked up to the UNIX system. You may need to ask your instructor or computer center where the default `lpr` printer is located.

This next command prints two files to a specific printer.

`lpr -Phplaser myfile myfile2`⏎

This example would attempt to print the files called *myfile* and *myfile2* to a printer on the UNIX system named *hplaser*. The -P is used to specify a printer different from the default printer. If your instructor or computer center informs you that you can use another printer in addition to the default printer, try the -P option on the `lpr` command.

Here is one more command. This example prints five copies of the file called *myfile* on a specific printer.

`lpr -Phplaser #5 myfile`⏎

This command is similar to the previous command except for the #5, which specifies that five copies of the file should be printed. You should make sure that the file prints correctly the first time before requesting multiple copies.

Checking the Printer Queue Status: lpq

When you send your file to the printer with the lpr command, it actually enters what is known as a print queue. The print queue is a temporary holding bin for print jobs until the printer becomes available. This allows people to send jobs to the printer and then continue working without having to wait for the printer to print their files.

If you are wondering where your jobs are in the print queue, you can use the lpq command. The lpq command has the following syntax: lpq -Pprinter. Note that if you specified a printer name when you used the lpr command, you need to specify the same printer name when you use the lpq command. Here is an example of this.

```
zard:~$ lpr -Phplaser testit.c
zard:~$ lpq -Phplaser
waiting for hplaser to become ready (offline ?)
Rank   Owner      Job Files                             Total Size
1st    sjames       0  testit.c                             70 bytes
zard:~$
```

You can see that you get quite a bit of information back from the lpq command. In this case, the job I sent is the first one in the queue (from the rank column). You can also see who owns the job, the job number (or ID), the job name, and the size of the job in bytes (1 byte = 1 character).

Cleaning up Print Jobs: lprm

There will be times when you send the wrong job to the printer and want to cancel it, or maybe you want to print a file, but it's time for you to leave and you don't want your printout laying around. These are perfect opportunities to use the lprm command, which removes jobs that you own from the print queue. The lprm command has the following syntax: lprm -Pprinter jobnumber. As before, if you named a specific printer in the command line of the lpr command, you must use the same printer name in the lprm command. The jobnumber is the ID of the job listed in the lpq command.

Here's how I could delete the job that I sent to the printer in the preceding example.

```
zard:~$ lpq -Phplaser
waiting for hplaser to become ready (offline ?)
Rank   Owner      Job Files                             Total Size
1st    sjames       0  testit.c                             70 bytes
zard:~$ lprm -Phplaser 0
dfA000Aa00218 dequeued
cfA000Aa00218 dequeued
zard:~$ lpq -hplaser
no entries
zard:~$
```

I first used the lpq command to learn the job number; in this case, the job number is 0. I then issued the lprm command with the 0 job number. UNIX then displays some informational messages telling me that my job was removed. When I perform a follow-up lpq, no entries are in the queue.

Try It

In this Try It! you explore how to print files.

1. Learn what printers are available to you, their names, and their locations. Your instructor or computer center should have this information.

2. Print a file to each of these printers using the lpr command. Make sure your file prints out.

3. Send a file and then remove it from the queue. This will require the use of the lpr, lpq, and lprm commands.

2-7 FILE OWNERSHIP AND PERMISSIONS

Remember the first ls -l command we examined in Section 2-2? It displayed a lot of letters in the left field of the listing. These letters indicate the permissions of the files and directories that were being listed. As you will learn in this section, file permissions and ownership are important UNIX security concepts.

UNIX is a fairly secure operating system. The owner of any file or directory has the ability to decide who else on the UNIX system can access that file. The owner can also decide what type of access is appropriate for various individuals.

UNIX security is built around the idea that three types of folks can access a file or directory.

- The *owner* of that file
- Anyone who is in the same *group* as the file owner
- The *world*, that is, anyone on the UNIX system

The *ownership* settings are displayed for each file and directory whenever you enter an ls -l command, as shown here.

```
zard:~$ cd ~
zard:~$ ls -l
total 10
drwx------    2 sjames    users            1024 Jun 20 13:10 Mail/
-rwxr-xr-x    1 sjames    users            3933 Jun 23 09:29 a.out*
drwxr-xr-x    2 sjames    users            1024 Jul  2 02:30 povray/
drwxr-xr-x    2 sjames    users            1024 Jul  5 12:17 render/
drwxr-xr-x    2 sjames    users            1024 Jul  5 12:37 scottstuff/
-rw-r--r--    1 sjames    users              70 Jun 23 09:29 testit.c
drwxr-xr-x    2 sjames    users            1024 Jun 27 11:21 xball/
zard:~$
```

The first field of the listing has a lot of d's, r's, w's, and x's in it. These provide information on the permissions of the files that I own. You can tell that I own the files and directories from the information provided in the third field (*sjames*). The fourth field indicates that I am in the *users* group.

Now let's get back to the first set of letters. A d in column 1 indicates that the entity is a directory (recall this from Section 2-2). The remaining nine letter spaces can contain up to three sets of rwx. The first rwx set refers to what the owner can do with the file or directory. The second rwx set tells what the group that the file or directory owner belongs to can do with the file. The third rwx set tells what the world can do with the file. In

CHAPTER 2 FUNDAMENTAL UNIX COMMANDS   **33**

other words, the first letter provides special information, such as the d
that indicates a directory, and the rest of the characters indicate what the
owner, group, and world can do with the file or directory.

Here is what each of the letters mean.

r   Indicates read access (the individual can read the file or directory)
w   Indicates write access (the individual can write to the file or
    directory)
x   Indicates execute access (the individual can run the program)

If you look at my /Mail directory, you can see that only I (the owner)
have read, write, and execute access to the directory. This makes sense
since I don't want anyone else doing anything to my mail. The program
a.out can be read, written to, and executed by me, but it can be only read and
executed by everyone else. Again, this makes sense since I might want other
people to be able to run my programs, but not to be able to change them.

Suppose, though, that I want to change permissions on a file or directory that I own. This is accomplished through the change mode command,
chmod, which has a syntax of chmod *permissions file/directory*.

The easiest way to deal with permissions is in their octal number form.
Permissions are identified by a three-digit number ranging from 000 to
777. The first number represents the rights of the owner, the second number represents the rights of the group, and the third number represents
the rights of the world. Each number is constructed by adding up the permissions you want to grant from the following list:

> 4=read access
> 2=write access
> 1=execute access

Now you can see that the range has to be between 0 and 7; 0 indicates
no rights, and 7 indicates read, write, and execute access. Here's the full list.

0 + 0 + 0 = 0—No rights	`---`
0 + 0 + 1 = 1—Execute access	`--x`
0 + 2 + 0 = 2—Write access	`-w-`
4 + 0 + 0 = 4—Read access	`r--`
0 + 2 + 1 = 3—Write and execute access	`-wx`
4 + 0 + 1 = 5—Read and execute access	`r-x`
4 + 2 + 0 = 6—Read and write access	`rw-`
4 + 2 + 1 = 7—Read, write, and execute access	`rwx`

Let's try changing permissions for some of the items in my home directory. Let's change *a.out* so that I have full access to it and my group can
read and execute it.

```
zard:~$ chmod 750 a.out
```

Let's set up the *xball* directory so that only I can access it.

```
zard:~$ chmod 700 xball
```

Here's an `ls` listing of the results.

```
zard:~$ ls -l
total 10
drwx------      2 sjames     users       1024 Jun 20 13:10 Mail/
-rwxr-x---      1 sjames     users       3933 Jun 23 09:29 a.out*
drwxr-xr-x      2 sjames     users       1024 Jul  2 02:30 povray/
drwxr-xr-x      2 sjames     users       1024 Jul  5 12:17 render/
drwxr-xr-x      2 sjames     users       1024 Jul  5 12:37 scottstuff/
-rw-r--r--      1 sjames     users         70 Jun 23 09:29 testit.c
drwx------      2 sjames     users       1024 Jun 27 11:21 xball/
zard:~$
```

File permissions and ownerships are something that you need to exercise a little caution with. If you accidentally set your account so that everyone is given full access, all of your files could be viewed, or worse, deleted by other folks. Use chmod sparingly to avoid this trouble.

2-8 REDIRECTION AND PIPES

Redirection and pipes allow you to send the output of a command to someplace other than the screen.

Redirection

Redirection simply redirects the output of a command. This is done by using >, which is the redirection operator. For example, if I want to print out a copy of the information that is in my home directory, I can use redirection to accomplish it.

```
zard:~$ ls -l > myhomedir
zard:~$ ls -l myhomedir
-rw-r--r--      1 sjames     users        516 Jul  5 13:52 myhomedir
zard:~$
```

The first line executed is the workhorse: `ls -l` normally sends output to the screen, but the > character tells UNIX to take the output of the `ls` command and send it to the file called *myhomedir,* which the command creates. Note that if the file that you are redirecting to already exists, it will be overwritten. You can remember which way the redirection is occurring by viewing the > as an arrow rather than as a greater-than sign.

The second `ls` shows that, sure enough, a new file called *myhomedir* has been created. Here are the contents of that file.

```
zard:~$ cat myhomedir
total 10
drwx------      2 sjames     users       1024 Jun 20 13:10 Mail/
-rwxr-x---      1 sjames     users       3933 Jun 23 09:29 a.out*
-rw-r--r--      1 sjames     users          0 Jul  5 13:52 myhomedir
drwxr-xr-x      2 sjames     users       1024 Jul  2 02:30 povray/
drwxr-xr-x      2 sjames     users       1024 Jul  5 12:17 render/
drwxr-xr-x      2 sjames     users       1024 Jul  5 12:37 scottstuff/
-rw-r--r--      1 sjames     users         70 Jun 23 09:29 testit.c
drwx------      2 sjames     users       1024 Jun 27 11:21 xball/
zard:~$
```

Now that I have my home directory information in a file, I can print it using the `lpr` command.

Another redirection operator is >>. This redirector tells UNIX to append the output to an existing file. Let's try putting the contents of the *povray* directory at the end of the *myhomedir* file we just created.

```
zard:·$ ls -l povray >> myhomedir
zard:~$ cat myhomedir
total 10
drwx------    2 sjames    users         1024 Jun 20 13:10 Mail/
-rwxr-x---    1 sjames    users         3933 Jun 23 09:29 a.out*
-rw-r--r--    1 sjames    users            0 Jul  5 13:52 myhomedir
drwxr-xr-x    2 sjames    users         1024 Jul  2 02:30 povray/
drwxr-xr-x    2 sjames    users         1024 Jul  5 12:17 render/
drwxr-xr-x    2 sjames    users         1024 Jul  5 12:37 scottstuff/
-rw-r--r--    1 sjames    users           70 Jun 23 09:29 testit.c
drwx------    2 sjames    users         1024 Jun 27 11:21 xball/
total 1669
-rw-rw-r--    1 sjames    users       360450 Jun 27 10:56 POVBIN_0.GZ
-rw-rw-r--    1 sjames    users       321982 Jun 27 10:56 POVBIN_1.GZ
-rw-rw-r--    1 sjames    users       121132 Jun 27 10:56 POVDOC_2.GZ
-rw-rw-r--    1 sjames    users        80476 Jun 27 10:56 POVINC_2.GZ
-rw-rw-r--    1 sjames    users        14033 Jun 27 10:56 POVRAY_2.REA
-rw-rw-r--    1 sjames    users       456404 Jun 27 10:56 POVSCN_2.GZ
-rw-rw-r--    1 sjames    users       167232 Jun 27 10:56 POVSRC_0.GZ
-rw-rw-r--    1 sjames    users       168586 Jun 27 10:56 POVSRC_1.GZ
zard:~$
```

Remember to use >> when you want to add information to an existing file; the single > operator creates a new file or overwrites an existing one.

Pipes

Like the redirection operator, a *pipe* also redirects output, but instead of sending the output of a command to a file, it sends the output of a command as the input of a second command. The pipe symbol is | (on some computers, the symbol is ¦).

Here's one use of a pipe: Many times `ls -l` produces more than one screenful of information. Wouldn't it be nice if you could use the `more` command to view that information? Through the use of a pipe you can.

```
zard:~$ cd /usr/bin
zard:/usr/bin$ ls -l | more
total 9601
lrwxrwxrwx  1 root  root      14 Jun 20 08:32 X11 -> /usr/X11R6/bin/
lrwxrwxrwx  1 root  root       4 Jun 20 07:10 [ -> test*
-rwxr-xr-x  1 root  bin    89596 Oct 12  1995 a2p*
-rwxr-xr-x  1 root  bin     6173 Aug 14  1995 ansi2knr*
-rwxr-xr-x  1 root  bin    21405 Aug 22  1995 answer*
-rwxr-xr-x  1 root  bin     1681 Oct 16  1995 apropos*
-rwxr-xr-x  1 root  bin    34284 May 22  1995 ar*
-rwxr-xr-x  1 root  bin    17668 May 22  1995 as*
-rwxr-xr-x  1 root  bin    65034 Jun  3  1995 as86*
-rwsr-xr-x  1 root  bin    17432 Oct 16  1995 at*
lrwxrwxrwx  1 root  root       2 Jun 20 07:05 atq -> at*
lrwxrwxrwx  1 root  root       2 Jun 20 07:05 atrm -> at*
lrwxrwxrwx  1 root  root       4 Jun 20 07:05 awk -> gawk*
```

```
-rwxr-xr-x  1 root  bin    16508 Oct 15  1995 banner*
-rwxr-xr-x  1 root  bin     4665 Aug 14  1995 basename*
lrwxrwxrwx  1 root  root       9 Jun 20 07:05 bash -> /bin/bash*
lrwxrwxrwx  1 root  root       2 Jun 20 07:05 batch -> at*
-rwxr-xr-x  1 root  bin     9328 Oct 16  1995 bban*
-r-xr-xr-x  1 root  bin    48433 Aug 14  1995 bc*
-rwxr-xr-x  1 root  bin       35 Aug  7  1995 bdftops*
-rwxr-xr-x  1 root  bin     4701 Aug 14  1995 bigram*
--More--
```

The /usr/bin directory is usually a huge directory on most UNIX systems (at least more than one screenful of information). I simply piped the output of the ls command to the more command. more behaves exactly as it did when it was used to look at the contents of a file. The only difference is that the listing doesn't indicate what percentage of the output has been viewed. The reason for this is that more simply doesn't know how big the total output of the directory listing will be since the ls command is still executing.

Try It

This Try It! examines redirection and piping.

1. Redirect the output of your UNIX system's */usr/bin* directory.

    cd ~ ⏎
    ls -l /usr/bin > binout ⏎

2. Display a long listing and notice how screenfuls of information scroll by.

    cat binout ⏎

3. Pipe the cat command through more.

    cat binout | more ⏎

4. Pipe the output of the ls command directly to the printer.

    ls -l | lpr ⏎

2-9 GETTING HELP WITH THE man PAGES

UNIX provides a fairly exhaustive online reference system. This help system is known as the manual, or man, pages. Almost every command that you can think of is located in the man system. To use man, simply type **man command**. The output of man is automatically sent to the more command so that you can see each screenful of information. Here's an example of man ls.

```
zard:~$ man ls
LS(1V)              USER COMMANDS              LS(1V)

NAME
  ls - list the contents of a directory

SYNOPSIS
  ls [ -aAcCdfFgilLqrRstu1] filename ...
[:]
```

```
DESCRIPTION
  For each filename which is a directory, ls list the con-
  tents of the directory; for each filename which is a file,
  ls repeats its name and any other information requested.  By
--More--(8%)
```

The preceding output shows you the name of the command, a synopsis, or summary, of all option switches available for the command, and a description of the command. If you continue to page through the output from the man command, you would find explanations and examples of each option switch.

SUMMARY

This chapter introduced you to the most basic UNIX commands. You can login and logout of your UNIX system and change your password. You can now create, remove, rename, copy, view, and print files. You can work with *vi* to perform file-editing tasks. You can even perform some intermediate-level tasks, such as performing print queue management, changing file permissions, and using redirection and piping. Finally, you should be able to use the UNIX man pages to get help on UNIX commands.

In the next chapter of this module, you will learn how one UNIX computer can communicate with another.

Key Words

Absolute path	more
cat	mv
cd	Ownership
chmod	passwd
cp	Permissions
Directory	Pipe
Executable files	prompt
Files	pwd
head	Redirection
Home directory	Relative path
Logging in	rm
logout	rmdir
lpq	tail
lpr	Text editor
lprm	Username
ls	vi text editor
man	Wildcard characters
mkdir	

Exercises

1. Using the man command, write down the NAME and SYNOPSIS lines from the more command.

2. Create a new text file with *vi* called *engr*. Enter the following list of words, one per line: **aeronautical**, **electrical**, **environmental**, **industrial**, **manufacturing**, and **mechanical**.

3. Print the text file created in Exercise 2.

4. Use *vi* to modify the text file created in Exercise 2. Add **computer** to the list in its proper location. Save your work and print this file.

5. Create a directory called *mywork* in your home directory. Copy the *engr* file to the *mywork* directory. Confirm that the copy worked correctly.

6. Rename the *engr* file in your home directory to *mydata*.

7. Use relative pathing and the ls command to examine the contents of the directory that is directly above your home directory.

8. Redirect the output of Exercise 7 to a file called *dirlist*, which should be located in your home directory. Print this file.

9. Using *vi*, edit your *mydata* file. Add your name and the name of the file to the first line of the file. Save your work.

10. Write down what the proper command line would be to print five copies of your *mydata* file to a printer named *inkjet*.

11. Append a long listing of the contents of your *mywork* directory to your *mydata* file using redirection. Print the *mydata* file.

12. Remove the *mywork* directory.

13. Redirect a long listing of your home directory directly to a printer using piping. Write down the command that you used.

14. Using absolute pathing, redirect a long listing of all the files in the */etc* directory on your UNIX system to a file in your home directory called *lastone*. Print this file.

3 UNIX Connectivity and the Outside World

Networking The ability for computers to "talk" to one another is quite an amazing thing if you think about it. You have the ability to connect to another computer almost anywhere in the world through a series of wires, fiber optic cables, satellite feeds, cellular networks, and microwave transmissions. This ability is considered by many to be one of the greatest achievements of modern times. We often take for granted what it takes to be able to communicate with other machines; in fact, many times we hear about computer communications only when the network is "down."

Since UNIX is such a powerful and flexible operating system, it is not surprising to find that it is used in most modern computer-controlled communications systems. In fact, the majority of computers that make up the Internet are UNIX-based systems. The emergence of computer communications has been one of the driving forces behind the operating system's success.

INTRODUCTION

This chapter examines how to use UNIX to communicate with other computers that may be located anywhere from the lab next door to halfway around the world. First you will learn how to find information regarding other computers and computer users with which you can communicate. Then you will learn how to send electronic mail, or e-mail. This chapter next gives you an overview of how to use *telnet* to connect to remote computers and *ftp* to retrieve remote files. The chapter concludes with an examination of some of the resources available on the Internet.

3-1 FINDING INFORMATION REGARDING OTHER USERS AND UNIX HOSTS

To communicate with other UNIX systems, you need information on the other UNIX computers that you can access. These other computers may provide some service for you that you do not have on the UNIX system you normally use. These service providers are called *hosts*.

In addition to finding out what other computers you can communicate with, you often need to try to find some information about other users. Knowing the electronic name of another user is critical if you want to correspond with that user through electronic mail.

This section will examine the tools available to you in the quest for this information.

Finding out Who's on Your System: who, w, and whoami

The who, w, and whoami commands all return information about users who are on your local UNIX system.

The who command provides a list of users currently logged on to the system. Let's take a look at this command.

```
zard:~$ who
larnold   ttyp0    Sep  3 08:49 (arial222.det.so)
vjames    tty1     Sep  3 09:31
sjames    ttyp1    Sep  3 09:30 (192.138.137.203)
zard:~$
```

You can see from the information returned in this example that currently three people are logged on to the system: *larnold, vjames,* and *sjames.* The next field of information provides the number of the particular terminal, or tty, that each user is using. Each user logged in is assigned a tty number by the system. The next two fields provide the date and time that each user logged in to the system. The last field shows where each user logged in from. You'll notice that user *vjames* doesn't have anything in the last column, whereas the other two users do. This is because user *vjames* is logged on from the UNIX computer itself, whereas the other two users have logged on from some location remote to the UNIX computer.

The w command provides information very similar to the who command. I personally believe that the command should have been called *what* since it provides information about each user in addition to what each user is doing. Here's an example.

```
zard:~$ w
 9:39am  up 2 days,  8:35,  3 users,  load average: 0.00, 0.00, 0.00
User     tty      from            login@  idle  JCPU  PCPU  what
larnold  ttyp0    arial222.det.so 8:49am    45              -tcsh
vjames   tty1                     9:31am     2              -bash
sjames   ttyp1    192.138.137.203 9:30am                     w
zard:~$
```

The first line returned from the command contains statistics about the UNIX system itself. In this case, it shows the current time, how long the computer has been on (or how long it's been since it was last rebooted), the number of users currently on the system, and the load average. The load average is a set of three numbers that show how busy the computer is; the higher the numbers, the busier the computer. The numbers may vary from system to system.

The next several lines reproduce that same information that was received from the who command, with the addition of four new columns. The *idle* column tells how long each user has been inactive. The *JCPU* and *PCPU* columns tell how long a user's job has been running. We'll be examining jobs in the next chapter. The last column tells what command or job each user is executing.

The whoami command tells you who you are logged in as.

```
zard:~$ whoami
sjames
zard:~$
```

The whoami command can also be typed as who am i. This command isn't terribly exciting, but some users have the ability to either login under different usernames or change from one username to another.

Finding User Information: finger and whois

The preceding section examined how to find out information about who was logged onto your local UNIX computer. The *finger* and *whois* commands allow you to get information on users located outside your own computer system.

The finger command works on both your local system and on other host computers. Let's run the command on user *sjames,* who is local to the system.

```
zard:~$ finger sjames
Login: sjames                          Name: Scott James
Directory: /home/sjames                Shell: /bin/bash
On since Tue Sep  3 09:30 (EST) on ttyp1 from 192.138.137.203
Mail last read Mon Sep  2 23:30 1996 (EST)
Plan:
I don't have a clue, much less a plan...
zard:~$
```

You'll notice that the command returns a lot of information. The value of some of it is questionable though. You can see that user *sjames*'s real name is Scott James. You are also provided with the name of *sjames*'s home directory and the particular shell that he uses. (Remember from Chapter 1 that the shell is what allows a user to interact with the computer.) The next line of information tells you the last time that *sjames* logged in to this computer and from where. You then learn the last time that *sjames* read his mail. The last entry is the user's plan, in which the user can provide any information he or she wants. If you want to create your own plan file, you simply need to use a text editor such as *vi* to create a file called *.plan*.

That was the first use for `finger`. You can also use `finger` with a host computer's name to find information about everybody who is logged in. Let's try this on another computer.

```
zard:~$ finger @nova.gmi.edu
[nova.gmi.edu]
Login       Name              TTY        Idle   When    Where
pbiatek   Paul Biatek        *pts/16       3d Fri 15:50  corvette.gmi.edu
sjames    Scott James         pts/23      16 Tue 10:05   zard.delpheus.com
real1142  John Patrick Reale  pts/34         Tue 10:20   198.110.0.127
erhu0945  Kimberly Rae Erhuan pts/24      22: Mon 11:54  blazer.gmi.edu
zard:~$
```

You can see that the `finger` command actually returns a lot of the same type of information as the who command. The nice thing about `finger` is that it works on remote computers (including those on the Internet). You only need to supply *@hostname* to the `finger` command; *@hostname* is the full name of a remote computer. You can then get detailed information about any of these users by using the `finger` command and supplying the *username@hostname* information. Let's see what *sjames*'s `finger` information on *nova* looks like.

```
zard:~$ finger sjames@nova.gmi.edu
[nova.gmi.edu]
Login: sjames                        Name: Scott D. James
Directory: /faculty/sjames           Shell: /bin/csh
On since Tue Sep  3 09:30 (EST) on ttyp1 from 192.138.137.203
Mail last read Tue Sep  3 12:30 1996 (EST)
Plan:
    No Plan.
zard:~$
```

The whois command is similar to the `finger` command in that it is used to return information about a particular user. The primary difference is that it looks to Internic organization for this information, meaning that you don't have to know the hostname of where the user is located. *Internic* is the organization responsible for giving out Internet Protocol, or IP, addresses for hostnames that are on the Internet. Every hostname must have a unique IP address. The *IP address* tells computers where to send information. Every communication taking place on the Internet will have two addresses: the IP address of the source computer and the IP address of the destination computer. All IP addresses are in the form of xxx.xxx.xxx.xxx, where the x's are numbers. In reality, an IP address is all that's required for communication to take place on the Internet; a host-name is a shortcut so that users don't have to remember the IP addresses. You don't actually need to concern yourself with IP addresses, but you should know what they are since almost every book on the Internet, and many on UNIX, mentions them.

Let's assume that I don't know what the hostname is for the UNIX computer that user *sjames* uses. If he has registered his information with Internic, I will be able to find him (and his host's name) via the whois command. Let's try it.

```
zard:~$ whois sjames
  [rs.internic.net]
James, Scott D. [Mr.] (SJ105)              sjames@nova.gmi.edu
  GMI Engineering & Management Institute
  1700 West Third Avenue
  Flint, MI  48504
  810.762.9859

  Record last updated on 13-Oct-92.

The InterNIC Registration Services Host contains ONLY Internet Information
(Networks, ASN's, Domains, and POC's).
Please use the whois server at nic.ddn.mil for MILNET Information.
zard:~$
```

From the returned information, you can see that *sjames*'s host computer is *nova.gmi.edu*. Note that not all UNIX computers have the whois command available.

Try It

This Try It! will allow you to test the finger and whois capabilities of your computer.

1. Find out if you have access to the whois command. If so, see if your instructor is in the whois database. (If your instructor is not listed, tell him or her to get registered!) The command should be in the following format.

   whois *your-instructor's-username* ⏎

2. Use the finger command to get some almanac information from user *copi* at host *oddjob.uchicago.edu*. The command should be

   finger copi@oddjob.uchicago.edu ⏎

Checking the Status of a Host Computer: ping

You can use the *ping* command to see if a given hostname is accessible. If ping doesn't return anything, it's safe to assume that the host machine is down for some reason. You can stop the ping command after you've received some replies by pressing (CTRL)-C. Here's a sample of the command.

```
zard:~$ ping nova.gmi.edu
PING nova.gmi.edu (192.138.137.2): 56 data bytes
64 bytes from 192.138.137.2: icmp_seq=0 ttl=255 time=1.8 ms
64 bytes from 192.138.137.2: icmp_seq=1 ttl=255 time=1.7 ms
64 bytes from 192.138.137.2: icmp_seq=2 ttl=255 time=1.6 ms
64 bytes from 192.138.137.2: icmp_seq=3 ttl=255 time=1.7 ms
64 bytes from 192.138.137.2: icmp_seq=4 ttl=255 time=1.6 ms

--- nova.gmi.edu ping statistics ---
5 packets transmitted, 5 packets received, 0% packet loss
round-trip min/avg/max = 1.6/1.6/1.8 ms
zard:~$
```

You can see that information was successfully sent to *nova* and received. You know this by looking at the second to last line before the prompt, which states that five packets were transmitted, five packets were received, and there was 0% packet loss. You can conclude from this that *nova* is alive.

Looking up Host Computer Information: nslookup

As already stated, there is a unique IP address for each hostname. Sometimes you may have an IP address but no corresponding hostname. The *nslookup* command can help you find the hostname. The nslookup command requires that either an IP address or a hostname be supplied. If the command can find the information given, it will report with both the hostname and IP address. For example, here's what the command returns when an IP address is supplied.

```
zard:~$ nslookup 192.138.137.2
Server:  nova.gmi.edu
Address:  192.138.137.2

Name:    nova.gmi.edu
Address:  192.138.137.2
zard:~$
```

Here's the nslookup command again, only this time, the hostname is supplied.

```
zard:~$ nslookup nova.gmi.edu
Server:  nova.gmi.edu
Address:  192.138.137.2

Name:    nova.gmi.edu
Address:  192.138.137.2
zard:~$
```

Attempting Text-Based Communication in Real Time: `talk`

The `talk` command allows two users on UNIX systems to "talk" to each other simultaneously. Actually, the two users can type and see each other's typing simultaneously. The two users do not have to be on the same system; they can be anywhere in the world. However, both users do need to be logged on. The `talk` command uses the following syntax: `talk` *username@hostname*. If the user is on the same system as you are, you don't need the *@hostname* part.

Let's try talking to user *larnold* on my local system.

```
zard:~$ talk larnold

 [Your party is not logged on]




------------------------------------------------------------------




zard:~$
```

The `talk` screen shows that the user I was trying to talk to wasn't logged on to my system, so I got the message `Your party is not logged on`. Let's try the command again, to user *vjames,* who is logged on to host *nova.gmi.edu.*

```
zard:~$ talk vjames@nova.gmi.edu
```

As soon as I type this command, I see the initial `talk` screen and the message `Waiting for your party to respond`. User *vjames* sees a message that says `talk: connection requested by sjames@zard.delpheus.com. Reply with talk sjames@zard.delpheus.com.`. When user *vjames* types the `talk` reply, her screen will split, and we can simultaneously type to each other. My conversation appears in the upper half, and *vjames*'s conversation appears in the bottom half of my screen.

```
[Connection established]
Hey V, Just wanted to see what you were doing.




-----------------------------------------------------------------

I'm busy running audits right now, can we talk later?
```

When either party wants to hang up, that user simply presses 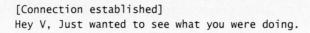CTRL-**C**.

3-2 USING E-MAIL

Electronic mail, or *e-mail,* is one of the greatest innovations to come out of the computer age. You can send a message at your convenience, as short or as long as you want, to virtually anyone, anywhere, for less than the cost of a postage stamp. Sending e-mail requires two items: the address of the person to whom you want to send e-mail and the message that you want to send.

Using the Standard UNIX E-Mail Command: `mail`

UNIX provides a basic e-mail package called *mail.* Here's how you send a message via *mail.* To begin, you type the `mail` command followed by the *username@hostname* address of the person to whom you want to send the mail. If the user is on the same system as you are, you don't have to include the *@hostname* portion. Once you have entered the command, you simply type your message. Some UNIX systems may ask you for the subject of the e-mail message; if yours does, just type a one-line summary of the message. The basic *mail* program is a quick-and-dirty approach to e-mail, so don't expect any fancy features such as word wrapping. You will need to enter returns where you want them. When you are finished typing your message, put a period on a line by itself; that will quit the *mail* program and send the message.

Here is an example of a *mail* message.

```
zard:~$ mail vjames@nova.gmi.edu
Subject: Quotas…
Hi V!
```

```
I was wondering if you have the system audit information back
yet.  I am very curious to see what the numbers are.

Thanks,
Scott
.
```

Now the *mail* program will send my message to user *vjames* at host *nova.gmi.edu*. If she is not on the system at the time the e-mail message is delivered, she will receive the message You have new mail the next time she logs on. If she does happen to be on the system at the time the mail is delivered, she will see the same message appear on her screen.

Let's assume that *vjames* reads the message and decides to e-mail a reply to me. I will see something like this.

```
zard:~$
You have new mail in /var/spool/mail/sjames
```

At this point, I can enter the mail command to read the message.

```
zard:~$ mail
Mail version 5.5 6/1/90.  Type ? for help.
"/var/spool/mail/sjames": 3 messages 1 new
    1 jrbyte@math.cornell.  Thu Aug 15 12:30  20/956   "Re:  Question about y"
    2 ykron@defiant.gmi.ed  Fri Aug 23 11:25  32/1315  "Win 95 on Voyager"
N   3 vjames@nova.gmi.edu   Tue Sep  3 13:18  16/520   "Quotas"
&
```

The *mail* program then shows me a list of all the messages that are in my mailbox. Notice that the last message listed has an N in front of it, indicating that this is a new message that I haven't read yet. Also notice that the last line contains &, which is the *mail* program's prompt. If I want to read a message, I simply need to enter the number of the message I want to read.

```
&3
Message 3:
From vjames@nova.gmi.edu Tue Sep  3 13:18:54 1996
Date: Tue, 3 Sep 1996 13:18:53 -0400
From: V James <vjames@nova.gmi.edu>
To: sjames@defiant.gmi.edu
Subject: Quotas

Scott,

I haven't got all of the numbers collected yet.  They should
be available by late this afternoon.  I hope that is soon enough.

V.

&
```

Again, I am left at the & prompt. If I want to, I can now look at other messages or enter a different *mail* command. I want to delete this message, so I enter the command **d**. Then I ask the *mail* program to show the subject lines of the messages again, this time using the **h** command.

```
& d
& h
    1 jrbyte@math.cornell.  Thu Aug 15 12:30  20/956    "Re: Question about y"
    2 ykron@defiant.gmi.ed  Fri Aug 23 11:25  32/1315   "Win 95 on Voyager"
&
```

The message was indeed deleted. I can now enter the **q** command to exit the *mail* program and to return to the UNIX system prompt.

```
& q
zard:~$
```

Note that there is a difference between the q command and the x command in *mail*. The q command quits the program; any messages marked as deleted will be gone the next time that you enter the *mail* program. The x command simply exits the program; any changes you've made such as messages marked for deletion will be disregarded, and the next time that you enter *mail*, everything will be back to the way it was.

Table 3-1 lists the commands that are usually available from the *mail* program.

Table 3-1   mail Commands

Mail Command	What It Does
+	Goes to the next message
–	Goes back one message
d	Deletes the message just displayed
h	Lists the headers of the messages
p	Redisplays the message
q	Quits the mail program, putting only undeleted messages back into the mail system
s *file*	Saves the message to the specified filename
x	Exits the mail program, undoing any changes you made
?	Displays the mail commands

Using Menu-Driven E-Mail Packages

Most UNIX systems today have abandoned the archaic method of standard UNIX *mail* in favor of a more user-friendly menu-driven approach. You will need to check with your instructor to determine if your system has a menu-driven e-mailer installed. Your school may have *elm*, *pine*, or one of the other popular e-mailers loaded on your UNIX system. Here is an example of the e-mailer called *elm*.

```
zard:~$ elm
```

```
        Mailbox is '/var/spool/mail/sjames' with 3 messages [ELM 2.4 PL24]


->N  1   Sep 3  V James        (17)   Quotas
     2   Aug 23 Yan Kron       (32)   Win 95 on Voyager
     3   Aug 15 J.R. Byte      (20)   Re:  Question about your internetwor
```

$$\left[\vdots \right]$$

```
          |=pipe, !=shell, ?=help, <n>=set current to n, /=search pattern
    a)lias, C)opy, c)hange folder, d)elete, e)dit, f)orward, g)roup reply, m)ail,
      n)ext, o)ptions, p)rint, q)uit, r)eply, s)ave, t)ag, u)ndelete, or e(x)it

Command:
```

The really nice thing about this e-mailer is that everything is menu driven. Almost everything that you might want to do is available from the menu. The program will also prompt you for any information that it needs.

To read a message, you use the arrow keys ⊕ and ⊕ to move the arrow pointer (->) up or down to the message that you want to read and then press the ⏎ key. Notice that an N appears in front of the first message to indicate that it is a new message.

Now to read message 1, I simply press ⏎.

```
Message 1/3  From V James                       Sep 3, 96 01:18:53 pm -0400

Return-Path: vjames@nova.gmi.edu
Date: Tue, 3 Sep 1996 13:18:53 -0400
To: sjames@defiant.gmi.edu
Subject: Quotas

Scott,

I haven't got all of the numbers collected yet.  They should
be available by late this afternoon.  I hope that is soon enough.

V.
```

$$\left[\vdots \right]$$

```
Command ('i' to return to index):
```

After reading the message, I am prompted to enter a command to the mailer. If I press **i**, I will be taken back to the main screen. At that point, I can enter another command, such as **d** for delete.

```
     Mailbox is '/var/spool/mail/sjames' with 3 messages [ELM 2.4 PL24]


     D  1   Sep 3  Val James          (17)   Quotas
        2   Aug 23 Yan Kron           (32)   Win 95 on Voyager
        3   Aug 15 J.R. Byte          (20)   Re:  Question about your internetwor
   [⋮]
        |=pipe, !=shell, ?=help, <n>=set current to n, /=search pattern
   a)lias, C)opy, c)hange folder, d)elete, e)dit, f)orward, g)roup reply, m)ail,
    n)ext, o)ptions, p)rint, q)uit, r)eply, s)ave, t)ag, u)ndelete, or e(x)it

Command:
```

Notice that message 1 has a **D** in front of it to indicate that it is marked for deletion. If I want to send a short message back to *vjames,* all I need to do is press **m** for mail. I will be prompted for a username, subject, and other folks who should receive a copy, and then I will be placed into an editor such as *vi.*

```
Mailbox is '/var/spool/mail/sjames' with 3 messages [ELM 2.4 PL24]


     D  1   Sep 3  Val James          (17)   Quotas
        2   Aug 23 Yan Kron           (32)   Win 95 on Voyager
        3   Aug 15 J.R. Byte          (20)   Re:  Question about your internetwor
   [⋮]
        |=pipe, !=shell, ?=help, <n>=set current to n, /=search pattern
   a)lias, C)opy, c)hange folder, d)elete, e)dit, f)orward, g)roup reply, m)ail,
    n)ext, o)ptions, p)rint, q)uit, r)eply, s)ave, t)ag, u)ndelete, or e(x)it

Command: mail
User: vjames@nova.gmi.edu
Subject: Quota info...
Copies to:
```

After I supply the information, the screen clears, and I am in my editor, where I can type my message.

```
V.

Thanks for the message.  This afternoon is fine.

Scott
   [⋮]
And now: s
     e)dit message, h)eaders, c)opy, i)spell, !)shell, s)end, or f)orget
File /tmp/snd.1968 saved.
```

After I type my message and save it, the e-mailer gives me the choice of editing the message before I send it, sending it as is, or not sending it. In this case, I type **s** for send to send the mail. Then from the index screen, I select **q** to quit the **elm** program.

Try It

This Try It! lets you try the e-mail procedures you have learned in this section. Send a message to the following *username@hostname* address: *almanac@oes.orst.edu*. If you are prompted for a subject line, leave the subject line blank. The message itself should simply say **send quote**.

If you are using standard UNIX mail, your screen should look like this.

```
mail almanac@oes.orst.edu ↵
Subject: ↵
send quote ↵
. ↵
```

If you have access to an alternative e-mailer, use that e-mailer to send the message to the same address.

In either case, after a little bit, you should receive an e-mail message back that contains a quotation from an almanac.

Some Thoughts on E-Mail Privacy and Etiquette

E-mail is not private. Any time you send an e-mail message, it is going to end up somewhere. If you send it to the wrong address, the intended recipient will not receive it, so the postmaster (the person who administers the e-mail system) on some computer will end up with it. You can think of e-mail as like a postcard, not a sealed letter. The gist of this is that you shouldn't send anything you wouldn't want others not to see. If you receive e-mail that you wouldn't want anyone else to view, delete it.

The following three issues affect the legality of the e-mail you send.

- It is illegal to transfer copyrighted materials through e-mail.
- You can be found guilty of libel, or the slandering of a person's character, via e-mail.
- Some materials that are not copyrighted are still illegal to transfer through e-mail, such as some types of pornography.

There are also some generally accepted rules of e-mail etiquette to follow when sending e-mail:

- Read and reply to your e-mail frequently.
- Make sure your messages are properly spelled and grammatically correct.
- Keep your message to the point.
- If you are replying to a message, briefly paraphrase what it is that you are replying to.
- Send messages only to those who need to receive them.

3-3 CONNECTING TO OTHER COMPUTERS

In this section, you will learn about two types of programs for connecting to other computers: *telnet,* which enables you to login to a remote computer, and *ftp,* which enables you to transfer files from a remote computer. Both of these programs are text based and have been around for some time. Newer communication software exists; however, many UNIX users still prefer these programs because they are fast and efficient.

Connecting to Remote Computers: telnet

telnet is a program available on most UNIX computers that allows you to login to a remote computer just as if you were sitting at that remote computer. *telnet* requires either the hostname or the IP address of the computer to which you want to connect.

The following example shows how to connect through *telnet* from my local machine *zard* to *nova.gmi.edu,* which is remote from my location. I start by entering the **telnet** command followed by the address of the computer I want to connect to.

```
zard:~$ telnet nova.gmi.edu
Trying 192.138.137.2...
Connected to nova.gmi.edu.
Escape character is '^]'.


UNIX(r) System V Release 4.0 (nova)


Only authorized users are allowed on this system, and use the
resources as explained in the Computer Usage Policy of GMI.

login:
```

After the login: prompt, I need to enter my username and then my password on *nova.gmi.edu.* If I successfully enter this information, I will be allowed onto the system.

```
login: sjames

Password:

Welcome to nova.gmi.edu.  Last login 3-Sep-96  14:06:11

helpdesk@nova Attention users: If you have any questions, concerns, or need
help, send mail to helpdesk@nova for a quick response.

Please run 'soft-up' for information on packages maintained by ellis.
You can access the GMI CWIS or Homepage (or any other) by running lynx at the
nova prompt.

SCHEDULED DOWNTIME: Fridays from 7:00 to 8:00 am will be reserved for
preventive maintenance and nova may be down.

You have mail.
nova{sjames}1%
```

The returned information shows that I have successfully connected from my local UNIX computer to a remote UNIX computer via *telnet.*

Once you login to a remote system in this way, you gain access to everything that would be available to you if you were actually sitting at the remote computer. You can use all of the UNIX commands that you have looked at so far. You can even ask the remote system to print out files for you, and those files will be printed on a printer at the remote location.

telnet gives UNIX users a considerable amount of power since users can access any computer that is available on the Internet for which they have an account. Once the user is logged in, the resources located on the remote computer become available for use.

To end a *telnet* session, simply **logout** of the remote computer. You will then be placed back on your local computer.

```
nova{sjames}2% logout
Connection closed by foreign host.
zard:~$
```

Here you can see that I logged out of *nova* and was returned to *zard*, where I started.

The `telnet` command has a second format in which a port number is supplied: `telnet` *hostname portnumber.* A port number indicates the location of a specific service on a remote host. For example, the University of Michigan has a geography server available on port 3000 at hostname *martini.eecs.umich.edu.* Let's make the connection:

```
zard:~$ telnet martini.eecs.umich.edu 3000
Trying 141.213.11.44...
Connected to martini.eecs.umich.edu.
Escape character is '^]'.
# Geographic Name Server, Copyright 1992 Regents of the University of Michigan.
# Version 8/19/92.  Use "help" or "?" for assistance, "info" for hints.
.
```

If you were to use the online help, you would learn that at the . prompt, you simply need to enter the zip code of the city for which you want information.

```
.
48415
0 Birch Run
1 26145 Saginaw
2 MI Michigan
3 US United States
F 45 Populated place
L 43 15 03 N  83 47 39 W
P 1196
E 635
Z 48415

.
quit
Connection closed by foreign host.
zard:~$
```

You can see that among the information returned is the name of the city; the county, state, and country in which it is located in; the coordinates of the city; and the city's population and zip code. When you are done, you type **quit** to exit the server and return to the local computer.

Any time a computer address has a number after it, it is most likely a port number that will need to be provided on the `telnet` line.

Try It You can practice your *telnet* skills by getting Mountain Standard Time from an atomic clock. The hostname is *india.colorado.edu*, and the port number is 13.

Enter the following command:

> `telnet india.colorado.edu 13` ⏎

After the time is given, you will be automatically disconnected from the remote computer. You don't need to type any commands such as `quit` or `exit`.

Retrieving Files from Other Computers: `ftp`

ftp stands for file transfer protocol, which is exactly what this program is used for: to copy remote files to your local computer. *ftp* is available on most UNIX computers. *ftp* requires the hostname or IP address of the computer from which you want to transfer files. Once you have connected to the computer, you will need to login with a username and password.

Why would you want to copy files from one computer to another using *ftp*? There are many answers to this question: There is a ton of free software available for just about every computer system imaginable, but you need to get a copy of the software before you can use it; or you may find some data files that you want to use in a research project, but the files are located on a computer across the country; or you may just want to transfer files among school, work, and home (assuming all three computers have *ftp* capability).

Although you have to login to the computer you want to use for *ftp* communication, you may not need to have an account on that computer. Thousands of sites are known as public, or anonymous, *ftp servers*. To use these, when you are prompted for a username, type `anonymous`. When you are prompted for a password, type your full electronic address (*username@hostname*).

If you try logging in to the computer as username `anonymous` with your electronic address as the password, and you get the login prompt again, the computer you are trying to access is not an anonymous *ftp* server. The only people who can access that particular computer have accounts on the computer.

Once you have logged in, you will see the `ftp>` prompt, from which you issue commands. Table 3-2 provides a list of valid *ftp* commands.

Table 3-2   ftp Commands

ftp Command	What It Does
ascii	States that you want to retrieve something in text mode
bin	States that you want to retrieve something in binary mode
cd	Changes directories on the remote computer
dir	Lists the contents of a directory; similar to ls -l
get *filename*	Sends the specified file to your local computer
hash	Displays # marks while files are being transferred
help	Displays a list of FTP commands
lcd	Changes directories on the local computer
mget *wildcard*	Sends multiple files to the local computer
mput *wildcard*	Sends multiple files to the remote computer
prompt	Toggles the prompt mode on or off for mget and mput operations
put *filename*	Sends the specified file from your local computer to the remote computer

The following example shows how to use *ftp* to connect to a computer at Oakland University located in Rochester, Michigan. I want to get a copy of the MS-DOS antivirus package called *F-Prot*. I begin by typing the **ftp** command followed by the address of the computer I want to connect to.

```
zard:~$ ftp oak.oakland.edu
Connected to oak.oakland.edu.
220 oak.oakland.edu FTP server (Version wu-
2.4(9) Wed May 3 15:02:49 EDT 1995) ready.
```

I have just accessed the Oakland computer. I don't have an account on it, but it is a public *ftp* server, so I will enter anonymous as my username and *sjames@zard.delpheus.com* as my password (remember the password won't show up as it is typed).

```
Name (oak.oakland.edu:sjames): anonymous
331 Guest login ok, send your complete e-mail address as password.
Password:
230-
230-                          Welcome to
230-                  THE OAK SOFTWARE REPOSITORY
230-          A service of Oakland University, Rochester Michigan
230-
230- If you have trouble using OAK with your ftp client, please try using
230- a dash (-) as the first character of your password -- this will turn
230- off the continuation messages that may be confusing your ftp client.
230- OAK is a UNIX machine, and filenames are case sensitive.
230-
230- Access is allowed at any time.  If you have any unusual problems,
230- please report them via electronic mail to archives@Oakland.Edu
230-
230- You are user #329 out of 400 maximum users on Wed May 24 12:14:28 1995.
230-
230- Oak is also on the World Wide Web, URL: http://www.acs.oakland.edu/
oak.html
230-
230- File searching is now available!  Example command:  site exec index 4dos
230-
230-Please read the file README
230-  it was last modified on Fri Mar 24 18:59:19 1995 - 61 days ago
230 Guest login ok, access restrictions apply.
```

I'm now logged in to the computer system, so now I will look around. I will use the di r command to do this.

```
ftp> dir
200 PORT command successful.
150 Opening ASCII mode data connection for /bin/ls.
total 1258
-rw-r--r--   1 w8sdz    OAK            0 Nov 13  1994 .notar
drwxr-x---   2 root     operator    8192 Dec 31 16:44 .quotas
drwx------   2 root     system      8192 Dec 30 19:16 .tags
-rw-r--r--   1 jeff     OAK      1093470 May 24 03:20 Index-byname
-r--r--r--   1 w8sdz    OAK         1237 Mar 24 18:59 README
drwxr-xr-x   3 w8sdz    OAK         8192 May 19 17:53 SimTel
d--x--x--x   3 root     system      8192 Jan 19 20:26 bin
d--x--x--x   2 root     system      8192 Jul 30  1994 core
drwxr-x---   2 cpm      OAK         8192 Nov 21  1994 cpm-incoming
d--x--x--x   5 root     system      8192 Dec 30 05:15 etc
drwxrwx---   2 incoming OAK         8192 May 24 11:54 incoming
drwxrwx---   2 25913    OAK         8192 Apr 23 10:50 nt-incoming
drwxr-xr-x   3 w8sdz    OAK         8192 Apr 13 19:46 pub
drwxr-xr-x  15 w8sdz    OAK         8192 Apr 13 19:46 pub2
drwxr-xr-x   8 w8sdz    OAK         8192 May  3 13:24 pub3
drwxr-xr-x   3 w8sdz    OAK         8192 May 19 17:53 simtel
drwxr-xr-x   2 jeff     OAK         8192 Apr 17  1994 siteinfo
drwx------  46 w8sdz    OAK         8192 May 22 21:42 w8sdz
226 Transfer complete.
1133 bytes received in 0.45 seconds (2.5 Kbytes/s)
```

I happen to know that all of Oakland's MS-DOS programs are located in the *SimTel* directory, so I will change directories using the cd command.

```
ftp> cd SimTel
250-The files in this directory tree are a mirror of SimTel, the Coast to
250-Coast Software Repository (tm).  Please read README.COPYRIGHT for
250-information on distribution rights.
250-
250-Please read the file README.COPYRIGHT
250-  it was last modified on Sun Apr 23 01:32:42 1995 - 31 days ago
250-Please read the file README.MIRRORING
250-  it was last modified on Thu Apr 27 12:49:22 1995 - 27 days ago
250 CWD command successful.
ftp> dir
200 PORT command successful.
150 Opening ASCII mode data connection for /bin/ls.
total 32
-rw-r--r--    1 w8sdz      OAK           172 Jan 28 15:05 .message
-rw-r--r--    1 w8sdz      OAK             0 Jan 28 15:05 .notar
-rw-r--r--    3 w8sdz      OAK          4605 Apr 23 01:32 README.COPYRIGHT
-rw-r--r--    3 w8sdz      OAK          1632 Apr 27 12:49 README.MIRRORING
drwxr-xr-x 221 w8sdz      OAK          8192 May 22 01:27 msdos
drwxr-xr-x  11 djgruber OAK           8192 May 20 02:57 nt
drwxr-xr-x  84 w8sdz      OAK          8192 May 23 23:21 win3
226 Transfer complete.
459 bytes received in 0.011 seconds (41 Kbytes/s)
```

The listing shows the *msdos* directory, where all the MS-DOS programs are stored. I want to change to that directory. Again, I will use the **cd** command.

```
ftp> cd msdos
250-This MS-DOS collection is a mirror of SimTel, the Coast to Coast
250-Software Repository (tm).  Questions about or comments on this
250-collection should be sent to w8sdz@SimTel.Coast.NET.
250-
250-Please read the file README.COPYRIGHT
250-  it was last modified on Sun Apr 23 01:32:42 1995 - 31 days ago
250-Please read the file README.MIRRORING
250-  it was last modified on Thu Apr 27 12:49:22 1995 - 27 days ago
250-Please read the file README.descriptions
250-  it was last modified on Sun Apr 23 01:38:53 1995 - 31 days ago
250-Please read the file README.dir-list
250-  it was last modified on Mon May 22 01:24:32 1995 - 2 days ago
250-Please read the file README.file-formats
250-  it was last modified on Sun Apr 23 01:40:24 1995 - 31 days ago
250-Please read the file README.how-to-upload
250-  it was last modified on Sun Apr 23 01:35:51 1995 - 31 days ago
250-Please read the file README.simtel-cdrom
250-  it was last modified on Fri May 12 12:36:58 1995 - 12 days ago
250 CWD command successful.
```

The *msdos* directory contains several hundred subdirectories. However, I know that the name of the subdirectory I'm looking for is *virus,* so I will use the **cd** command again to change to that directory.

```
ftp> cd virus
250 CWD command successful.
```

I know that the *F-Prot* program is stored in a file that starts with *fp* and has a version number following it. I will look for any files that start with *fp*.

```
ftp> dir fp*.*
200 PORT command successful.
150 Opening ASCII mode data connection for /bin/ls.
-rw-r--r--   1 w8sdz      OAK         737527 Aug  22 16:04 fp-224a.zip
226 Transfer complete.
remote: fp*.*
66 bytes received in 0.0051 seconds (13 Kbytes/s)
```

That's the file I want. It's a binary file, so I'll change to binary mode and download the file.

```
ftp> bin
200 Type set to I.
ftp> get fp-224a.zip
200 PORT command successful.
150 Opening BINARY mode data connection for fp-224a.zip (737527 bytes).
226 Transfer complete.
local: fp-224a.zip remote: fp-224a.zip
737527 bytes received in 118 seconds (6 Kbytes/s)
```

There are two types of files on the computer: *text files,* which humans can read, and *binary files,* which is stuff that only a computer could love. Text files usually have names like *Readme.txt* or *READ.ME,* or anything with a *.txt* extension. Just about everything else is binary: *.jpg, .gif, .zip, .arc, .exe,* and so on. You need to make sure that you download binary files in binary mode. If you're not sure which mode to use, select bin to be safe. Text files download correctly in binary mode, but binary files will not be complete if you download them in text (ascii) mode.

I downloaded nearly three quarters of a megabyte in just under two minutes. I now have a copy of the *F-Prot* program on my computer and I can do what I want with it. Now I'll stop the *ftp* program with the quit command.

```
ftp> quit
221 Goodbye.
```

 Try It   Practice your **ftp** skills by retrieving the file called *README* from the **ftp** site *oak.oakland.edu.* You will need to connect as user anonymous and type your *username@hostname* for the password.

1. Login to the *ftp* site:

```
ftp oak.oakland.edu ↵
Connected to oak.oakland.edu.
220 oak.oakland.edu FTP server (Version wu-2.4(9) Wed May 3 15:02:49 EDT 1995)
ready.
Name (oak.oakland.edu:sjames): anonymous ↵
331 Guest login ok, send your complete e-mail address as password.
Password: your-username@hostname ↵
230-
230-                           Welcome to
230-                  THE OAK SOFTWARE REPOSITORY
230-         A service of Oakland University, Rochester Michigan
230-
```

```
230- If you have trouble using OAK with your ftp client, please try using
230- a dash (-) as the first character of your password -- this will turn
230- off the continuation messages that may be confusing your ftp client.
230- OAK is a UNIX machine, and filenames are case sensitive.
230-
230- Access is allowed at any time.  If you have any unusual problems,
230- please report them via electronic mail to archives@Oakland.Edu
230-
230- Oak is also on the World Wide Web, URL: http://oak.oakland.edu/
230-
230- To search for files, use the command: quote site exec index filename
230-
230-Please read the file README
230-  it was last modified on Fri Mar 22 15:07:51 1996 - 146 days ago
230 Guest login ok, access restrictions apply.
```

2. Now that you're on the system, look for the *README* file.

```
ftp>dir ↵
200 PORT command successful.
150 Opening ASCII mode data connection for /bin/ls.
total 1874
-rw-r--r--    1 w8sdz    OAK            0 Nov 13  1994 .notar
drwxr-x---    2 root     operator    8192 Dec 31  1994 .quotas
drwx------    2 root     system      8192 Dec 30  1994 .tags
-rw-r--r--    1 jeff     OAK      1826389 Aug 15 03:19 Index-byname
-r--r--r--    1 w8sdz    OAK         1386 Mar 22 15:07 README
drwxr-xr-x    2 jeff     OAK         8192 Apr 28 22:21 SimTel
d--x--x--x    3 root     system      8192 Jan 19  1995 bin
d--x--x--x    2 root     system      8192 May  6 16:11 core
drwxr-x---    3 cpm      OAK         8192 Mar 22 16:46 cpm-incoming
d--x--x--x    6 root     system      8192 Aug 14 03:14 etc
drwxr-xr-x   10 jeff     OAK         8192 Jul 22 08:32 irc
drwxr-xr-x   16 w8sdz    OAK         8192 Jul 24 15:41 pub
drwxr-xr-x    2 jeff     OAK         8192 Apr 17  1994 siteinfo
drwx------   46 w8sdz    OAK         8192 Aug  5 19:48 w8sdz
226 Transfer complete.
879 bytes received in 0.13 seconds (6.6 Kbytes/s)
```

3. The file called *README* is listed; now copy it using the get command.

```
ftp>get README ↵
200 PORT command successful.
150 Opening ASCII mode data connection for README (1386 bytes).
226 Transfer complete.
local: README remote: README
1415 bytes received in 0.17 seconds (8 Kbytes/s)
```

4. You have the file, so type the **quit** command to stop the *ftp* program.

```
ftp> quit ↵
221 Goodbye.
```

5. You have a copy of the *README* file on your local computer. Use more to look at it, vi to edit it, or lpr to print it.

3-4 INTRODUCTION TO USING THE INTERNET'S RESOURCES

This chapter has referred to the Internet; now it's time to address this topic directly. So far you know that all hosts on the Internet have to have a hostname and a unique IP address assigned to them. You have looked at how to locate information on other computers and find other users, and how to connect to other computers through *telnet* and retrieve files through *ftp.* This section examines other resources that are commonly available on the Internet. You will have to check with your instructor or your school's computer center to determine whether you have access to these resources. This section focuses on three Internet services: UseNet News, gophers, and the World Wide Web. Bear in mind that this section is only a quick introduction to these services.

UseNet News: The Internet's Daily Press

For many Internet users, UseNet News is the reason they wanted access to the Internet. UseNet News is a collection of thousands of newsgroups. A newsgroup is an electronic version of a pushpin board, where UseNet News users can pin up information on a topic. Each newsgroup tries to keep all information within it pertaining to a particular topic. The beauty of UseNet News is that there are newsgroups dedicated to just about any topic you can think of. This gives you the ability to actively participate with other people who share the same interests as you. The other plus to using UseNet News is that you can post questions that you need answers to since there may be people who are experts reading your posts.

To use UseNet News, you must have a newsreader available, and it must be configured to point at a news server. A news server is nothing more than a host that has UseNet News articles on it. Several common UseNet News readers are used on UNIX systems: *nn, rn,* and *tin.* Most newsreaders are menu driven and pretty easy to use. Let's take a look at the *nn* reader.

I begin to read the news by typing **nn** on my computer.

```
zard:~$% nn
Connecting to NNTP server news.gmi.edu ...
Connecting to NNTP server news.gmi.edu ... ok (posting is allowed)
```

At this point, *nn* tries to connect to my news server, which is *news.gmi.edu.* Once it has connected to the server, I am shown the first newsgroup that I have subscribed to, or the first new newsgroup, whichever comes up first. Initially when you run *nn,* you will be subscribed to every newsgroup that is out there. If you view a newsgroup that you don't want to see again, press **U** to unsubscribe to it. Here's what the initial newsgroup looks like on my system.

```
Newsgroup: alt.3d                                Articles: 37 of 707/11

a Markus Valppu    108  !!! Look at here for A LOT OF FAST CASH !!!
b car               18  SCHEMERS AGAIN AND AGAIN
c Daniel Odulo      31  >
d idrum73@sover      2  >>
e idrum73@sover      2  >>
f Eric Kempter      57  >Bill Clinton
g Charles Durham    29  >>>NT 4.0 / Win 95 required for MH3D
```

```
h Darrick Coleman  10  Nirvana magazines i will buy
i Brinstar@wink    13  >PLEASE HELP THIS PREMATURE LITTLE GIRL
j Roberto-NY        7  Animated texture maps
k Jeremy Hamilton 246  Fast Money!!!!!!
l Secure1245        3  >what is the best 3d software and where to get it
m 240 SHorTy       89  >! MAKE MONEY BS
n VIDS              3  What happened to .SXP's in MAX
o Denis Guenette   89  ! MAKE MONEY$$ WITH MANY NEW FRIENDS
p Denis Guenette   89  ! MAKE MONEY$$$, FREE AND EASY
q AnimMaster        7  >MH3D Book/Manual
r A Bicalho        18  >Cyrix 6x86 and 3DStudio
s F B Ortega       41  >Stereoscopic Imaging & (Unrelated) 3D-Studio R4 for sale

-- 11:44 -- SELECT -- help:? -----Top 50%-----
```

This particular newsgroup is named *alt.3d* (look at the top line). The newsreader also lets me know that there are 37 articles I haven't read in this group (the newsreader shows you only new articles by default). There are a total of 707 new articles in all the 11 groups that I am subscribed to. The columns of information that are displayed include the letter of the news article, the author of the news article, the number of lines in the news article, and the subject of the news article. The very last line tells me that I am seeing the top half of the list of new articles in *alt.3d*. It also tells me that if I want help, I can press **?**. This is what the help screen looks like.

```
SELECT (toggle)                          MOVE
a-z0-9   Specified article        ,        Next menu line
x-y      Range x to y             /        Previous menu line
x*       Same subject as x        SPACE    Next menu page (if any)
.        Current article          < >      Prev/Next menu page
@ ~      Reverse/Undo all selections  ^ $  First/Last menu page
=regexp Matching subjects (=. selects all)
L/JJJJ   Leave/Change attributes  ( )      Open/Close Consolidated line
SHOW SELECTED ARTICLES
SPACE    Show (only when on last menu page)
Z        Show NOW, and return to this group afterwards
X        Show NOW, and continue with next group
GOTO OTHER GROUPS
X        Update current group, skip to next.  Y     Group overview
N P      Goto next/previous group.        ~/.nn/init:
G        Goto named group or open a folder.      Defines group
B A      Go back/forward in groups already read.  presentation sequence.
MISCELLANEOUS
U        Unsubscribe / Subscribe toggle  :man   Online manual
F R M    Follow-up/Reply/Mail            :help  More online help
S O W    Save articles                   !      Shell escape
:post C Post new article / Cancel current "      Change menu layout
:unshar :decode :patch  Unpack articles  Q      Quit nn
Hit any key to continue
```

Pressing any key returns me to the newsreader.

If I want to read an article, all I have to do is press the letter of that article. I can also select multiple articles on this page. To see the second page of the articles in *alt.3d,* I can press the spacebar. I will select two articles, **r** and **s**.

I could now press the (SPACE BAR) and select other articles from this group. When I reach the end of a group, all the articles that I have selected from that group will be displayed. I can also tell the newsreader that I want to see the two selected articles now, however, by pressing the **Z** key, as the help page indicates.

Here's the first article.

```
A Bicalho: >Cyrix 6x86 and 3DStudio                 Wed, 04 Sep 1996 00:55
moretti@zeus.csr.unibo.it (Carlo Moretti mat.1088) wrote:


>I heard about problems with 6x86.
>Anyone tried 3DS with the new Cyrix processors??

>Also PPro should have problems with 3DS v4.
>Is it true!?

Look for the Kinetix page. They've launched an upgrade for 3DS 4 to
run in the Ppro and 6x86 machines. It's in the downloads directory as
patch.
Haven't seen much documentation, but many people are having problems
with Ppro.


Good Luck



-- 11:55 --alt.3d-- 1 MORE --help:?--All--
```

The article pertains to a software package called *3D Studio*. The first line of the article tells me the author's name and the date the article was posted to the newsgroup. The last line from the newsreader lets me know that I have one more article to view. To see it, I press the spacebar.

```
F B Ortega: >Stereoscopic Imaging & (Unrelated) 3D-
Studio R4 for sale996 03:04
Robert J. Rosenblum wrote:
>
>     Does anyone have any experience with the stereoscopic imaging
> plug-in from vrex (or other if there is one *?*) I'd be very interested
> in hearing your feedback.
>
> Also!
>
> please post or write:
>
> max@noonanrusso.com
> or
> mr774@bard.edu

Hello Robert, nice to meet you here in news,
my name is Francisco Blanca(Paco), i come from Spain(MM-alaga),
iM-4m finishing Computer Science, here in MM-alaga, and i want
-- 11:56 --alt.3d-- LAST --help:?--Top 40%--
```

If you want to, you can press **S** to save an article you are viewing (you will be prompted for a name). Once you have saved the article, you can print it using the **lpr** command. I want to save the current article I am viewing.

```
F B Ortega: >Stereoscopic Imaging & (Unrelated) 3D-Studio R4 for sale996 03:04
Robert J. Rosenblum wrote:
>
>      Does anyone have any experience with the stereoscopic imaging
> plug-in from vrex (or other if there is one *?*) I'd be very interested
> in hearing your feedback.
>
> Also!
>
> please post or write:
>
> max@noonanrusso.com
> or
> mr774@bard.edu

Hello Robert, nice to meet you here in news,
my name is Francisco Blanca(Paco), i come from Spain(MM-alaga),
iM-4m finishing Computer Science, here in MM-alaga, and i want
Save on (+~|) +alt/3d
```

As soon as I pressed the **S** key, I was asked if I want to save the article to the *alt/3d* file that is already in my directory on my system. I simply press ↵, and a copy is stored on my local computer that I can now edit or print. If I wanted to save the file under a different name, I could have deleted the *alt/3d* that was displayed and simply entered the new name. You may be asked by the newsreader if it is okay to create a new file or group. You will see that message if you specify a new filename. Press **Y** for yes, and the file will be created and the message saved.

The other side of reading newsgroups is writing to them. You can post new articles to a group by typing **:post**, or you can reply to an existing article by pressing **R**. Both options are very similar to using an e-mailer in that you will be put in an editor where you can type your message. Once you've composed your message, it will eventually be posted on UseNet News—assuming that you have the ability to post articles; not all Internet news servers do. Note that there will be some lag time until your message is circulated to all the different news servers. Let's look at how to post a message.

I begin by typing the **:post** command.

```
F B Ortega: >Stereoscopic Imaging & (Unrelated) 3D-
Studio R4 for sale996 03:04
Robert J. Rosenblum wrote:
>
>     Does anyone have any experience with the stereoscopic imaging
> plug-in from vrex (or other if there is one *?*) I'd be very interested
> in hearing your feedback.
>
> Also!
>
> please post or write:
>
> max@noonanrusso.com
> or
> mr774@bard.edu

Hello Robert, nice to meet you here in news,
my name is Francisco Blanca(Paco), i come from Spain(MM-alaga),
iM-4m finishing Computer Science, here in MM-alaga, and i want
```
:post
```
POST to group
```
alt.3d
```
Subject:
```
3D Studio Max Files
```
Keywords:
Summary:
Distribution (default 'world')
```

Now, after entering the questions concerning which group to post to, the subject of the article I want to post, keywords for the article, summary of the article, and the distribution of the article, I can type my message.

```
Path: gmi.edu!sjames
Date:   4 Sep 96 16:14:23 GMT
Message-ID: <sjames.841853663@gmi.edu>
Newsgroups: alt.3d
Subject: 3D Studio Max Files...
Organization: GMI Engineering&Management Institute, Flint, MI
```

Does anyone know if the older 3d studio files are 100% compatible with the new Max version?

Thanks,

Scott James
```
~
```
$$[\vdots]$$
```
~
"/usr/tmp/nn.a25972" 8 lines, 204 characters
```

I am in *vi*, so when I am finished typing my message, I need to type **:qw!** to save my file. The newsreader then comes back with the following list of choices.

```
a)bort e)dit h)old m)ail p)ost r)eedit v)iew w)rite
Action: (post article)
```

I can press **p** to post the message, **e** to edit the message and make changes, or **a** to abort posting the message. I will press **p**, at which point I am shown this message.

```
Be patient!  Your new article will not show up immediately!
```

Then I am eventually returned to my newsreader. The last line shows that the article was posted.

```
F B Ortega: >Stereoscopic Imaging & (Unrelated) 3D-Studio R4 for sale996 03:04
Robert J. Rosenblum wrote:
>
>     Does anyone have any experience with the stereoscopic imaging
> plug-in from vrex (or other if there is one *?*) I'd be very interested
> in hearing your feedback.
>
> Also!
>
> please post or write:
>
> max@noonanrusso.com
> or
> mr774@bard.edu

Hello Robert, nice to meet you here in news,
my name is Francisco Blanca(Paco), i come from Spain(MM-alaga),
iM-4m finishing Computer Science, here in MM-alaga, and i want
-- 12:18 --alt.3d-- LAST --help:?--Top 40%--(Filed)--
Article posted
```

I can now press **Q** to quit and return to my UNIX prompt. Before returning me to the prompt, the newsreader lets me know that there are still articles that I have not read.

```
There are still 706 unread articles in 11 groups

zard:~$
```

gopher: A Menu-Based Information Browser

gopher is another interesting resource on the Internet. *gopher* allows you to access information on the Internet through a common menu interface. Instead of having to use *telnet* to go to various locations and use *ftp* to get text files from a remote computer, all you need to do is move through menus on the *gopher* system and press ⏎ when you find something that is of interest to you.

gopher sites contain a lot of varied information. The periodic table is available through *gopher*. There are electronic books such as the *CIA World Fact Book* and the *King James Bible* online. You can also find song lyrics and entire movie scripts through *gopher*.

To use *gopher*, you must have the appropriate software loaded on your UNIX system. I can access it simply by typing **gopher**.

```
zard:~$ gopher
Welcome to the wonderful world of Gopher!

Gopher has limitations on its use and comes without
a warranty.  Please refer to the file 'Copyright' included
in the distribution.

Internet Gopher Information Client 2.0 patch16
Copyright 1991,92,93,94 by the Regents of the University of Minnesota


Press RETURN to continue
```

Now that *gopher* has started, I can press the ⏎ key to bring up the main menu.

```
GMI Gopher Information Server Main Menu

 -->  1.   About This Gopher at GMI(Updated 3/5/95)
       2.   The GMI Undergraduate Catalog - 1994-1995 <HTML>
       3.   Academic Programs/
       4.   CSO Version of the GMI Phonebook <CSO>
       5.   UNIX Update - GMI/
       6.   Calendars and Schedules/
       7.   Computer Policy at GMI/
       8.   Computer Resources at GMI(lots of help)/
       9.   GMI Campus Organizations and People/
      10.   GMI Falcon Library Catalog <TEL>
      11.   General Interest - Non-GMI/
      12.   Scholarly and Academic Resources/
      13.   Virtual Visitors' Center/
      14.   Select this if using a WWW browser and you opened gopher:..du/
            <HTML>


Press ? for Help, q to Quit
```

The last line tells you that you can press **?** to get help or **q** to quit the system. Like *nn, gopher* is quite friendly in helping you move around.

One other item of importance is the arrow pointer (-->) in front of option 1 on the menu. This is the *gopher* pointer, and you can move it to other locations by pressing the ⬆ and ⬇ arrow keys. If you want to choose a menu option, you can press ➡ to go into it or ⬅ to move out of it.

Any option on the menu that has a slash (/) after it has submenu choices. Let's choose option 11, `General Interest - Non-GMI`. (I can type the number, or I can press ⬇ to get to it.)

```
General Interest - Non-GMI

 -->  1.   Auroral Activity
       2.   Computer Software Archives/
       3.   Current Events/
       4.   Education/
       5.   Entertainment/
       6.   Flint Computer Resources - GFEC Hypertext Page <HTML>
       7.   Flint Local Weather Forecast
       8.   General Weather Forecast/
       9.   Libraries/
```

```
10. Miscellaneous Network Services/
11. Newspapers and Newsmagazines/
12. Online Books and Journals/
13. Other gophers/
14. Politics/
```

The option I selected was actually a submenu full of more choices. Let's look at choice 12, `Online Books and Journals`, which is also a submenu.

```
Online Books and Journals

 -->  1. Voice of America and Worldnet Television/
      2. A Collection on College Campus Newspapers <HTML>
      3. ACADEME THIS WEEK (Chronicle of Higher Education)/
      4. Annals of Improbable Research(also J.of Irreproducble Results)/
      5. Classics Collections (wiretap.spies.com)/
      6. Computer-Mediated Communication Magazine <HTML>
      7. EDUCOM Documents and News/
      8. Electric Mystics Guide/
      9. Electronic Journals/
     10. Electronic Publications and Resources/
     11. GTOnline from the Colorado City Gazette Telegraph <HTML>
     12. Journals at University of Michigan Library/
     13. Learned NewsWire 1.5 <HTML>
     14. On-Line College Papers (LA Tech Gopher)/
     15. Project Gutenberg/
     16. The Interpedia Project/
     17. Time-Warner Publications Online <HTML>
     18. WIRED Magazine/
```

I now have a lot of additional choices. One of the more interesting is option 15, `Project Gutenberg`, where copies of books such as the *King James Bible* are located.

Let's look at another example, where I get the local weather forecast for Flint, Michigan. I need to move back up to the previous submenu, `General Interest - Non-GMI` first, which I will do by pressing ⏎ once.

```
General Interest - Non-GMI

 -->  1. Auroral Activity
      2. Computer Software Archives/
      3. Current Events/
      4. Education/
      5. Entertainment/
      6. Flint Computer Resources - GFEC Hypertext Page <HTML>
      7. Flint Local Weather Forecast
      8. General Weather Forecast/
      9. Libraries/
     10. Miscellaneous Network Services/
     11. Newspapers and Newsmagazines/
     12. Online Books and Journals/
     13. Other gophers/
     14. Politics/
```

Now I need to select option 7 to get `Flint Local Weather Forecast`.

```
The Weather Machine // UofI Atmospheric Sciences

[There are a number of problems here and we are still experimenting
so I wouldn't set your bookmark here just yet.  You are welcome
to make use of the data in the meantime though. Comments welcome.]

Surface Reports For Stations In Michigan,US
        station  ceiling  sky      tmp dwpt wind  alt.  vis weather
        location  (ft)    cover             kts   in.   mi
        -------------------------------------------------------------
17Z 9/4/96:
FNT FLINT/BISHO  5500 scattered  82  58  W 04 30.03   4  haze


Press Return for Menu.
```

At this point, I will press ⏎ to return to the General Interest - Non-GMI submenu and then press **q** to quit *gopher* and return to my UNIX prompt.

The World Wide Web:
Putting the Internet at Your Fingertips

The *World Wide Web*, or WWW, is the fastest growing portion of the Internet. This is what all those weird-looking computer addresses that you see on television and newsprint advertisements are referring to. When someone says that they are "surfing the Internet," they are most likely browsing the World Wide Web. The World Wide Web is truly best experienced on a multimedia computer since it represents full-motion video graphics and stereo sounds as well as simple text.

Web browsers, which are used to look at the content of the pages that are placed on the Web come in two distinct types: text and graphical. *Text browsers*, such as *www* and *lynx*, allow users to view text content and retrieve files only. *Graphical browsers* allow users to more fully enjoy what the web has to offer, providing access to text, images, and sound with the simple click of a mouse. There are graphical browsers available for the UNIX platform, but these require that you use some form of X Windows. (Appendix B provides a brief overview of X Windows, which is somewhat similar in operation to Microsoft Windows on a PC.)

Although it is not nearly as interesting as surfing the Internet with a graphical browser, text browsing still allows you to get around and access information on the Web. Let's look at my department homepage through the eyes of *lynx,* which is a text browser.

```
zard:~$ lynx

IMSE at GMI   (p1 of 3)

                        Welcome To The IMSE Home Page
                                    at
                      GMI Engineering & Management Institute




                        Page is constantly being updated.


        _____


                [1]About Industrial & Manufacturing Engineering

                    [2]Undergraduate Catalog 1994 - 1995

                [3]Manufacturing Systems Engineering Curriculum

                    [4]Industrial Engineering Curriculum

-- press space for next page --
  Arrow keys: Up and Down to move. Right to follow a link; Left to go back.
 H)elp O)ptions P)rint G)o M)ain screen Q)uit /=search [delete]=history list
```

You don't see any of the nice graphics. There won't be any sound. Furthermore, moving around is not as simple as pointing and clicking with a mouse. You navigate as you do in *gopher,* using the arrow keys and reading the screen prompts for commands.

If you want to give *lynx* a new address to go to, you press **G**, for go. Let's tell *lynx* to go to *oak.oakland.edu* via *ftp*. Web browsers present every Internet service through the same convenient interface.

```
IMSE at GMI   (p1 of 3)

                        Welcome To The IMSE Home Page
                                    at
                      GMI Engineering & Management Institute




                        Page is constantly being updated.


        _____


                [1]About Industrial & Manufacturing Engineering

                    [2]Undergraduate Catalog 1994 - 1995

                [3]Manufacturing Systems Engineering Curriculum

                    [4]Industrial Engineering Curriculum

URL to open: ftp://oak.oakland.edu
  Arrow keys: Up and Down to move. Right to follow a link; Left to go back.
 H)elp O)ptions P)rint G)o M)ain screen Q)uit /=search [delete]=history list
```

As soon as I pressed the **G** button, a line popped up asking me for the URL (address) to go to. Since I want to use *ftp*, I need to enter **ftp:?//** and then the hostname. You can also use *telnet*, *ftp*, *gopher*, and *mailto* (to e-mail someone on the Internet).

As soon as I press ⏎ key after the address, the Oakland screen appears, and I can starting moving around.

```
Welcome  directory (p1 of 2)


                              Welcome

_____



                          Welcome to
                 THE OAK SOFTWARE REPOSITORY
        A service of Oakland University, Rochester Michigan

If you have trouble using OAK with your ftp client, please try using
a dash (-) as the first character of your password -- this will turn
off the continuation messages that may be confusing your ftp client.
OAK is a UNIX machine, and filenames are case sensitive.

Access is allowed at any time.  If you have any unusual problems,
please report them via electronic mail to archives@Oakland.Edu

Oak is also on the World Wide Web, URL: http://oak.oakland.edu/

-- press space for next page --
  Arrow keys: Up and Down to move. Right to follow a link; Left to go back.
 H)elp O)ptions P)rint G)o M)ain screen Q)uit /=search [delete]=history list
```

Moving down a screen, I see a list of directories, identified by numbers, that I can change to.

```
Welcome  directory (p2 of 2)
 To search for files, use the command: quote site exec index filename

Please read the file README
  it was last modified on Fri Mar 22 15:07:51 1996 - 166 days ago
_____

Nov 13  1994   text/plain      [1].notar
Dec 31  1994   Directory       [2].quotas
Dec 30  1994   Directory       [3].tags
Jan 19  1995   Directory       [4]bin
May  6 16:11   Directory       [5]core
Mar 22 16:46   Directory       [6]cpm-incoming
Sep  4 13:23   Directory       [7]etc
Sep  4 03:19   text/plain      [8]Index-byname   1738Kb
Jul 22 08:32   Directory       [9]irc
Jul 24 15:41   Directory       [10]pub
Mar 22 15:07   text/plain      [11]README   1Kb
Apr 28 22:21   Directory       [12]SimTel
Apr 17  1994   Directory       [13]siteinfo
Aug 21 00:39   Directory       [14]w8sdz
Commands: Use arrow keys to move, '?' for help, 'q' to quit, '<-' to go back.
  Arrow keys: Up and Down to move. Right to follow a link; Left to go back.
 H)elp O)ptions P)rint G)o M)ain screen Q)uit /=search [delete]=history list
```

I'll select number 11, which is the same *README* file you copied earlier in a *ftp* Try It! exercise.

(p1 of 2)


```
                     Welcome to OAK.Oakland.Edu
                     THE OAK SOFTWARE REPOSITORY
            A service of Oakland University, Rochester Michigan

OAK.Oakland.Edu is a primary mirror of Simtel.Net, Keith Petersen's
world-wide distribution network for Shareware, Freeware, and Public
Domain programs for MS-DOS, Windows 3.x, and Windows 95.  To access, cd
to /pub/simtelnet.  If you would like to subscribe to a mailing list
that announces new uploads to the Simtel.Net collections see ms-news.txt
in subdirectory 00_info in any of the directories under /pub/simtelnet.

All MS-DOS, Windows 3.x, and Windows 95 files have been checked for viruses
with the latest virus scanning programs available at the time of upload.
Reasonable care has been taken for your protection but Oakland University
does not certify this software to be free of viruses, trojans or bugs.
Use at your own risk.

Changes in the directory heirarchy of the OAK Software Repository are
-- press space for next page --
  Arrow keys: Up and Down to move. Right to follow a link; Left to go back.
  H)elp O)ptions P)rint G)o M)ain screen Q)uit /=search [delete]=history list
```


Since it was plain text, *lynx* simply displayed it on my screen. But if I change into the *virus* directory and select the *F-Prot* program I downloaded earlier, watch what happens.


```
Nov 19  1988   Zip File        [57]file-crc.zip   53Kb
Jul 18  1988   Zip File        [58]filecrc.zip    39Kb
Mar 13  1988   Zip File        [59]filetest.zip   46Kb
May 20  1989   Zip File        [60]find1701.zip   18Kb
Sep 28  1989   Zip File        [61]fixcrime.zip   22Kb
Apr 17 23:51   Zip File        [62]fixutil6.zip   28Kb
Jul  1  1995   Zip File        [63]flsf106.zip    62Kb
Aug 22 17:04   Zip File        [64]fp-224a.zip    738Kb
Oct  7  1990   Zip File        [65]fshld15.zip    29Kb
Aug  6  1992   Zip File        [66]fsp_184.zip    46Kb
Feb 19  1992   Zip File        [67]hcopy15.zip    61Kb
Apr 20  1993   Zip File        [68]htscan20.zip   92Kb
Jul 18 20:13   Zip File        [69]i_m302a.zip    406Kb
Apr 12  1989   Zip File        [70]ibmpaper.zip   23Kb
Jun 16  1988   text/plain      [71]ibmprot.doc    10Kb
Jun  9  1989   text/plain      [72]identify.txt   19Kb
Mar 27  1988   text/plain      [73]immunity.txt   4Kb
Feb  6  1991   Zip File        [74]innoc.zip      2Kb
Dec 28  1987   Zip File        [75]inoculat.zip   5Kb
Sep  3  1995   Zip File        [76]iv-610.zip     421Kb
This file cannot be displayed on this terminal:  D)ownload, or C)ancel
 Arrow keys: Up and Down to move. Right to follow a link; Left to go back.
 H)elp O)ptions P)rint G)o M)ain screen Q)uit /
=search [delete]=history list
```

The third line from the bottom tells me that the file can't be displayed. This makes sense since it is binary. I'll select **D** to download it, which sends it via *ftp* to my local machine. I am then presented with the following options:

```
Lynx Download Options

                    Download Options (Lynx Version 2.5-GMI)

You have the following download choices.
Please select one:

[1]Save to disk
[2]Use Kermit to download to the local terminal
[3]Use Zmodem to download to the local terminal
[4]Use Xmodem to download to the local terminal
[ : ]
Commands: Use arrow keys to move, '?' for help, 'q' to quit, '<-' to go back.
 Arrow keys: Up and Down to move. Right to follow a link; Left to go back.
 H)elp O)ptions P)rint G)o M)ain screen Q)uit /=search [delete]=history list
```

I want to save the file to disk, so I will select option 1. I will then be prompted for a filename. By default, *lynx* uses the same name as what was sent via *ftp,* but you can change it if you want. Since I have the file, I press **Q** to quit *lynx* and return to my UNIX prompt.

As you can see, Web browsing is a powerful tool. You should also see that graphical Web browsing is the preferred choice.

SUMMARY

This chapter introduced you to some of the basic concepts of computer communications. You learned how to find information about other users through the w, who, whois, and finger commands. You also learned how to find out information about other UNIX computers by using the ping and nslookup commands. You saw how to communicate with other users through the talk program and whatever form of e-mail you have available. The chapter then showed you how to connect to remote computers via *telnet* and how to copy remote files via *ftp.* The chapter concluded with an introduction to a few of the more valuable resources that the Internet has to offer: UseNet News, *gopher,* and the World Wide Web.

In the next chapter of this module, you will learn more advanced operations that can be performed under UNIX. Compiling computer programs with C and Fortran will be examined. In addition, the creation of scripts, which are files with multiple UNIX commands, will be presented.

Key Words

Binary files	*pine*
elm	ping
E-mail	rn
finger	Servers
ftp	talk
gopher	*telnet*
Graphical browsers	Text browsers
Host	Text files
Internic	tin
IP address	w
lynx	who
mail	whoami
nn	whois
nslookup	World Wide Web

Exercises

1. Redirect the output of the w command to a file and print the file. Circle your username on the printed page.

2. Use the finger command to get a copy of your finger information. Redirect the output of the command to a file and print the file.

3. If you can access the Internet from your school, use the finger command to look at the address *@coke.elab.cs.cmu.edu*. What did you receive from the address?

4. Enter an nslookup command using your hostname. Write down the IP address for your host.

5. Use the talk command to converse with a friend or classmate. Write a paragraph or two describing your experience with the program.

6. Send a short e-mail message to your instructor telling him or her how much you like the class you're in.

7. Send a short e-mail message to a friend. Ask your friend to send a message back to you that contains the name of the class that he or she likes the best this term. Print this message.

8. Communicate via *telnet* from your UNIX computer to another computer on campus. Login to the computer, and then redirect the output of a who command to a file. Print this file.

9. If you are connected to the Internet, use *telnet* to go to the address *culine.colorado.edu 862*. Write a description of what you encountered there.

10. Use *ftp* to send a text file of your instructor's choice to your account. Edit the file and place your name at the top of it. Print this file.

11. If you have access to a newsreader, get on UseNet News, and print any three articles from three different newsgroups that you are interested in.

12. If you have access to *gopher,* and your school has a gopher server, retrieve some information of your instructor's choice. Print this information.

13. If you have access to a Web browser, go to *http://defiant.gmi.edu,* and print the Web page if you are able. If you can't print the page, comment on what information you found there.

14. If you have access to a Web browser, go to *http://www.yahoo.com.* This site provides a search engine. Enter some subject that you are interested in inside the search box. If the engine returns links pertaining to your interest, follow one of the links, and if possible, print the Web page at that link.

4

Becoming More Productive: Advanced UNIX Operations

Problem Solving with UNIX

Computer scientists and software engineers are always looking for ways to make the computer more intuitive and creative in its problem-solving abilities. Artificial intelligence (AI) is the area in computer science that best encompasses this phenomenon. We would like to think that computers can be as logical and sentient as Data in *Star Trek: The Next Generation.* The truth is that we are a long way from that point. Today, many artificial intelligence systems are based on what are called expert systems, which are a set of rules that an expert uses in trying to solve a problem. For example, if you have a cold and go to your doctor, the doctor usually asks you a series of questions that end up providing a diagnosis and treatment of your particular illness. If we can gather the rules that the doctor uses, we could make a computer mimic the doctor's role. A second area of AI involves programs that learn and adapt to input values. These types of systems are known as neural networks and genetic algorithms. These systems "learn" over time and have been used in predicting weather patterns and analyzing the stock market. Many types of AI systems have been developed on UNIX systems because of the speed and power of UNIX.

INTRODUCTION

This chapter examines some of the more advanced UNIX operations that engineers and scientists should be aware of and able to use. The chapter opens with a discussion of the use of programming language compilers under UNIX. It then presents commands for managing a variety of jobs, or processes, including commands to help you live within the quota of your allotted memory on the computer. The chapter proceeds with a discussion of various other UNIX commands and tools that are available and can assist in many housekeeping tasks. The chapter concludes with an examination of shell scripts.

4-1 USING PROGRAMMING LANGUAGE COMPILERS UNDER UNIX

Many introductory programming classes are taught on UNIX computers, so it is worthwhile to examine how to compile a program on a UNIX computer. Any program that is written in a high-level language such as *Pascal, C,* or *Fortran* must be converted into what is called an *object program.* Computers can't directly understand the text file source programs that you write, so you must use a *compiler* to convert these programs into binary object programs that the computer can execute.

Let's take a look at how to enter a simple Fortran program on the **vi** editor. This program must be typed in at least column 7 of the editor since columns 1 through 6 are reserved for line numbers and comments in the Fortran *programming language.* This section is not designed to teach you about programming languages, nor does it make any assumptions about your programming skills. You should just take each program for face value as it appears. Note that uppercase and lowercase letters and punctuation must be entered exactly as shown here.

```
PROGRAM MYPROG

INTEGER AGE
CHARACTER*10 NAME

PRINT *,'Hello, please type your name...'
READ *,NAME
PRINT *,'Thank you.  Please tell me your age...'
READ *,AGE
PRINT *,'----------------------------------------'
PRINT *,NAME,' IS ',AGE,' YEARS OLD'
PRINT *,'----------------------------------------'
END
```

After I typed this program, I saved it as *myprog.f.* The Fortran compiler expects all programs to end with a *.f* extension.

Now let's try to convert from the *source program* to an object program through the use of the Fortran compiler, which is called *f77* on most UNIX systems. The basic syntax of the command is f77 *filename.f.* If there are no errors in the source program, an object program called *a.out* will be created, which can then be run. Let's go ahead and try this.

```
zard:~$ f77 myprog.f
myprog.f:
 MAIN myprog:
zard:~$
```

Since there were no errors in my source code, the object program *a.out* was created. Let's check with the ls command.

```
zard:~$ ls -l a.out
-rwx------   1 sjames   faculty     14096 Sep  4 16:04 a.out*
zard:~$
```

Let's try and run it.

```
zard:~$ a.out
 Hello, please type your name...
Scott
 Thank you.  Please tell me your age...
28
 ----------------------------------------
 Scott      IS   28 YEARS OLD
 ----------------------------------------
zard:~$
```

The program works correctly: It asks for a user's name and age and then prints the information back out to the screen.

Since I don't really like the name *a.out,* I'll tell the compiler what I want the object program to be called. To do this, I need to add a -o *outputname* option to the f77 line.

```
zard:~$ f77 -o myprog myprog.f
myprog.f:
 MAIN myprog:
zard:~$
```

That told the compiler to create an object program called *myprog.* I can see if I was successful by using the ls command again.

```
zard:~$ ls -l myprog
-rwx------   1 sjames   faculty     14096 Sep  4 16:08 myprog*
zard:~$
```

Let's try to run the object program.

```
zard:~$ myprog
 Hello, please type your name...
Scott
 Thank you.  Please tell me your age...
28
 ----------------------------------------
 Scott      IS   28 YEARS OLD
 ----------------------------------------
zard:~$
```

It still works.

Note that although you can name the object program anything that you like, it is a good idea to choose a name similar to that of the source program. The only other point to concern yourself with is that the compiler overwrites the old object program each time you perform a compilation.

Now let's try writing the same program in the C programming language. This time I am going to put an error in the program to show you what happens when the compiler encounters one. Here's the buggy program.

```c
#include <stdio.h>
#include <strings.h>

main()
{
  int age;
  char name[10];

  printf("Hello, please type your name...\n");
  scanf("%s",name);
  printf("Thank you. Please tell me your age...\n");
  scanf("%d",&age);
  printf("-------------------------------\n");
  printf("%s is %d years old\n",name,age);
  printf("-------------------------------\n");
}
```

C doesn't care what column things begin in. I saved this program as *newprog.c.* The C compiler expects C programs to end in a *.c* extension. Now I'll try to create the object program. I need to use the C compiler command, which is *cc* on most UNIX systems.

```
zard:~$ cc -o newprog newprog.c
"newprog.c", line 11: newline in string literal
"newprog.c", line 12: syntax error before or at: scanf
zard:~$
```

The C compiler tells me there is an error on line 11, which there is because I forgot to put a double quotation mark before the end parenthesis on the second printf line in the program. Since there were errors, no output program was created.

```
zard:~$ ls -l newprog
newprog: No such file or directory
zard:~$
```

I will go back and fix the *newprog.c* program with *vi.* Here's the corrected copy.

```c
#include <stdio.h>
#include <strings.h>

main()
{
  int age;
  char name[10];
```

```
printf("Hello, please type your name...\n");
scanf("%s",name);
printf("Thank you. Please tell me your age...\n");
scanf("%d",&age);
printf("-------------------------------\n");
printf("%s is %d years old\n",name,age);
printf("-------------------------------\n");
}
```

I'll recompile it now. Then I'll check to make sure that the object program exists and execute it.

```
zard:~$ cc -o newprog newprog.c
zard:~$ ls -l newprog
-rwx------   1 sjames    faculty      5864 Sep  4 16:21 newprog*
zard:~$ newprog
Hello, please type your name...
Scott
Thank you. Please tell me your age...
28
-------------------------------
Scott is 28 years old
-------------------------------
zard:~$
```

The program now works fine since all the errors that were in the source program have been fixed.

Try It

In this Try It! you type a C program on your UNIX computer and try to compile it. There are no errors in this program, so if your compiler tells you that something is wrong, you will need to check closely what you entered. The source C program should be called *tryit.c*.

1. Type the following C program with whatever file editor you like to use:

```
#include <stdio.h>
#include <strings.h>

main()
{

  int num1, num2, total;
  char name[15];

  printf("Please tell me your name:\n");
  scanf("%s", name);
  printf("Please give me an integer number\n");
  scanf("%d", &num1);
  printf("And another\n");
  scanf("%d", &num2);

  total = num1 + num2;

  printf("%s, your numbers %d + %d = %d\n", name, num1, num2, total);
}
```

2. Make sure the last line of the file is blank (press ⏎ an extra time).

3. Save the file as *tryit.c.*

4. Compile the file with the following command:
   cc -o tryit tryit.c⏎

5. If there are any errors, you will need to use your file editor to fix the program. If there are no errors, run the program by typing **tryit**.

Here's a sample run, just so that you know the program works.

```
zard:~$ tryit
Please tell me your name:
Scott
Please give me an integer number
5
And another
10
Scott, your numbers 5 + 10 = 15
zard:~$
```

4-2 RUNNING JOBS IN THE BACKGROUND

You have already learned that UNIX is capable of running multiple jobs at the same time. This concept, called multitasking, was introduced in Chapter 1. A UNIX job is called a process. In addition to simply letting the computer run multiple processes itself, you can run multiple processes by placing them in the *background.*

So far, whenever you have typed a UNIX command, it has run in the *foreground.* This means that the results of the process appear on your screen, and your keyboard is usually tied up until the process is done running. For example, if you used the *telnet, ftp, lynx,* or *gopher* command in Chapter 3, you were stuck in that particular program until you told the program that you wanted to quit. This doesn't have to be the case, though, since you can move any program from the foreground into the background.

This section also examines other commands for working with UNIX processes. The ps command allows you to see what processes you have running. The *bg* and *fg* commands allow you to move between the foreground and the background. The jobs command allows you to display a list of processes that you have placed in the background. Finally, the kill command allows you to terminate processes.

Placing Processes in the Background: & and bg

There are essentially two ways to place a process in the background: starting a process with the &, which means run the process in the background, and suspending a process in the foreground and moving it to the background with bg. Let's take a look at both of these methods.

In Chapter 3, we looked at the *ftp* program, which allows us to copy files from remote computers. Normally, I start *ftp* and connect to the remote computer with everything happening in the foregound. If I add the & to the end of the ftp command, I immediately get my UNIX prompt back and can continue with other work.

```
zard:~$ ftp nova.gmi.edu &
[1] 3472
zard:~$ ls
Mail/        myprog*        myprog.f        newprog*        newprog.c
```

Instead of seeing the `ftp` login prompt, I got a set of numbers back ([1] 3472) and my system prompt. The 3472 is the system-assigned process identification number, or PID. Every process that is run on the computer has to have a unique number assigned to it. The UNIX system does this for you, so you don't have to worry about it. The [1] indicates that this is the first process that I have running in the background.

Notice that as soon as I get my system prompt back, I can start typing other UNIX commands.

Now let's take a look at the second method of getting jobs in the background, by suspending them.

```
zard:~$ ftp nova.gmi.edu
Connected to nova.gmi.edu.
220 nova FTP server (UNIX(r) System V Release 4.0) ready.
Name (nova.gmi.edu:sjames): sjames
331 Password required for sjames.
Password:
230 User sjames logged in.
ftp>
```

I am now on the remote machine, with everything happening in the foreground. If I want to put this `ftp` process in the background so that I can do other work, I need to suspend it and move it to the background. To suspend a process under UNIX, I press the (CTRL)-**Z** key combination. I now type the command **bg** to put the process in the background. Let's see what happens when I do this (you aren't going to see the special keystroke show up).

```
[2]+  Stopped                 ftp nova.gmi.edu
zard:~$ bg
[2]+ ftp nova.gmi.edu &
zard:~$
```

This screen tells me that the process has been suspended and is running in the background, which is the same effect I achieved by using &, except that I chose when to put this process in the background, whereas the & starts the process in the background. Notice that the last line shows the command I typed with the & appended to the end of it. I again have my system prompt, so I can start entering other commands.

Finding out What You Have Running: ps

With processes now running in the foreground and background, you may want to get a list of all the processes that you are running. The command for this is *ps*, which stands for process show. Here's an example.

```
zard:~$ ps
  PID TTY STAT  TIME COMMAND
 3452 pp0 S     0:00 -bash
 3485 pp0 T     0:00 ftp nova.gmi.edu
 3488 pp0 R     0:00 ps
zard:~$
```

The first column provides the process identification (PID) numbers for each of the processes that are running. The next three columns tell me the TTY number where the process is running, the status of the process, and the amount of CPU time each process has used. The final column lists the process or command name. Notice that the shell, which is my interface to the computer, shows up first as -bash. I then see my ftp process, which is running in the background, and the ps command, which I just issued.

Try It   Find out what processes you have running with the ps command. You should see at least two processes: your shell and the ps command. The command is **ps** ⏎.

Stopping Jobs: kill

There may be times when you try to logout of your UNIX system and you receive the following message.

```
zard:~$ logout
There are stopped jobs.
Zard:~$
```

If you were to type **logout** again, you would indeed be logged out. The question is what does this message mean? It's the UNIX system's way of telling you that you have jobs still running in the background. You should check what processes you have running with the ps command to ensure that something important isn't running in the background. In any case, you should get used to checking for processes you may have left running in the background and not relying on the UNIX system to do it for you.

You can stop any job by using the *kill* command. For example, here's how I stop the ftp process running in the background. First I enter the **ps** command to get the PID number. Then I perform the **kill** command.

```
zard:~$ ps
  PID TTY STAT  TIME COMMAND
 3452 pp0 S     0:00 -bash
 3485 pp0 T     0:00 ftp nova.gmi.edu
 3516 pp0 R     0:00 ps
zard:~$ kill -9 3485
[2]+  Killed                  ftp nova.gmi.edu

zard:~$ ps
  PID TTY STAT  TIME COMMAND
 3452 pp0 S     0:00 -bash
 3517 pp0 R     0:00 ps
zard:~$
```

An informational message from the system tells me that the job was indeed terminated. I can also see from the output of the second ps command that the ftp process was stopped.

Let's look at the kill command that I typed. The 3485 is the PID number of the process that I wanted to stop, but what is the -9 for? The -9 is what's known as a signal; in particular, this signal means that I want the job stopped immediately. There are other signals available, but -9 is the only one that we are going to concern ourselves with here. You should follow this syntax when using the kill command: kill -9 *PIDnumber*.

Switching from Process to Process: jobs, fg, and bg (again)

When you put multiple jobs in the background, you will sometimes want to switch from one job to another. This is done with the *jobs* command, which displays a list of everything you've put in the background. jobs is different from ps; whereas ps shows all processes, jobs shows only processes running in the background. I will put a couple of processes in the background and then get a listing of what's running.

```
zard:~$ telnet nova.gmi.edu &
[1] 3529
zard:~$ ftp nova.gmi.edu &
[2] 3530
zard:~$ jobs
[1]-  Stopped (tty output)     telnet nova.gmi.edu
[2]+  Stopped (tty input)      ftp nova.gmi.edu
zard:~$
```

Both processes that I placed in the background show up in the list. I can then choose which process I want by typing **%** and one of the bracketed job numbers. If I want to bring the *telnet* process to the foreground, I can type **%1**. I could then bring the *ftp* process to the foreground by typing **%2**, which effectively puts the *telnet* process in the background since only one process can be in the foreground at a time.

You will notice that there is a + sign by the *ftp* process. This indicates that this was the most recent of all the jobs running to be in the foreground. If I want to bring that job to the foreground, I can issue the command **fg**. To return it to the background, I would again need to suspend it with the (CTRL)-**Z** key combination and then enter the command **bg**.

In the following examples, I will use these commands to bring the *ftp* process to the foreground, suspend it and return it to the background, and then bring the *telnet* process to the foreground. First I list the jobs and bring the *ftp* process to the foreground.

```
zard:~$ jobs
[1]-  Stopped (tty output)     telnet nova.gmi.edu
[2]+  Stopped (tty input)      ftp nova.gmi.edu
zard:~$ fg
ftp nova.gmi.edu

331 Password required for sjames.
Password:
Login failed.
ftp>
```

Next I suspend the *ftp* process and return it to the background with the bg command.

```
[2]+  Stopped                  ftp nova.gmi.edu
zard:~$ bg
[2]+ ftp nova.gmi.edu &
zard:~$
```

Now, I bring the *telnet* job to the foreground.

```
zard:~$ %1
telnet nova.gmi.edu


UNIX(r) System V Release 4.0 (nova)


Only authorized users are allowed on this system, and use the
resources as explained in the Computer Usage Policy of GMI.

login: sjames
```

I could continue to hop back and forth between processes with the combination of the jobs, fg, and bg commands. It will take some practice to get proficient at this skill, but the work is definitely worth it since you will be able to run multiple processes and select which one you want to use.

4-3   SETTING PROCESS PRIORITIES: nice

At times you may find yourself running a job that is going to take quite a while to complete. You may want to change the process *priority* of the job so that it does not use as much of the system resources. You can do this with the *nice* command, which tells a process to run at a certain priority. The higher the nice number, the lower the priority of the process. The default for each process is set to 10. The values 1 through 19 are available for use to UNIX users.

Suppose that I want to send a file via *ftp* that is going to take quite a while. I can reduce the drain on the system resources by using the nice command. To do so, I start the process with a nice command tied to it.

```
zard:~$ nice -15 ftp nova.gmi.edu
Connected to nova.gmi.edu.
220 nova FTP server (UNIX(r) System V Release 4.0) ready.
Name (nova.gmi.edu:sjames): sjames
331 Password required for sjames.
Password:
230 User sjames logged in.
ftp>
```

When using the `nice` command, note that - is a command separator just like in `ls -al`; thus, the `nice` value was 15, not *minus* 15. Further, the valid range of `nice` values is different on some UNIX systems. Consult the man pages for help by entering **man nice**.

Monitoring the System Load: uptime

Another appropriate time to use the `nice` command is when the system load is getting quite high. The easiest way to see the system load is to use the *uptime* command.

```
zard:~$ uptime
 10:42am  up 4 days,  9:38,  2 users,  load average: 0.07, 0.03, 0.01
zard:~$
```

The last three numbers indicate the load average. You've seen that line before since it is the first line that is printed following the w command.

```
zard:~$ w
 10:44am  up 4 days,  9:39,  2 users,  load average: 0.02, 0.02, 0.00
User     tty      from             login@  idle  JCPU   PCPU  what
vjames   tty1                      9:11am  1                  -bash
sjames   ttyp0    192.138.137.203  9:13am        2           w
```

What do these numbers tell you? The first load average number indicates the *system load average* over the last minute, the second number indicates the load average over the last 5 minutes, and the third number indicates the load average over the last 15 minutes.

These numbers are relative to the system you are on. A load of 5 on one system may mean that it's not even "breaking a sweat," whereas a load of 5 on another system means things are going at a snail's pace. You need to ask your instructor or computer center what a medium load is for your particular UNIX system. If you see that the load is creeping up to that point, you may want to apply `nice` to any of your processes that are taking a lot of resources to help things out a bit.

 Try It Check your system load by typing **uptime** or **w**. Consult your instructor or computer center to determine what light, medium, and heavy load averages are for your system.

4-4 SCHEDULING PROCESSES

All UNIX systems have the ability to allow users to run processes at specific times, even when the user is not logged in or present on the system. This section will address two of those commands: *at* and *cron*.

Specifying When to Run a Process: at

UNIX systems have the ability to run processes when you tell them to with the at command. The basic syntax of the command is at *time command*. The time must be specified in 24-hour format. Let's tell the computer to display a directory of my account in one minute from the current system time, which we can get with the *date* command.

```
zard:~$ date
Thu Sep  5 10:51:06 EDT 1996
zard:~$ at 10:52 ls
zard:~$ date
Thu Sep  5 10:51:23 EDT 1996
zard:~$ date
Thu Sep  5 10:51:46 EDT 1996
zard:~$ date
Thu Sep  5 10:51:48 EDT 1996
zard:~$
zard:~$
Mail/     myprog*   myprog.f  newprog*   newprog.c
```

Try It

In this Try It! you will ask UNIX to perform a command five minutes from now.

1. Find out what the current system date and time is.

   date ⏎

2. Write the at command to display your directory in five minutes from the current time.

   at *time+5minutes* **ls** ⏎

   Be sure to replace *time+5 minutes* with an actual value.

Scheduling and Running Processes Automatically: crontab

The cron command, which is run by most UNIX systems automatically, is somewhat similar to the at command in that it allows you to run processes at the time you specify. The at command required you to type each process to be executed from the keyboard. The cron command allows a special file called the crontab to be created in which you enter the day and time that a specific job is to be run. The nice thing about cron is that once the *crontab* has been set up, you don't have to be logged in or even remember to type any commands. Once the UNIX system runs cron, it will look for *crontab* entries and execute the commands within them automatically.

Table 4-1 shows that a *crontab* file has six items that must be placed on each line of the file.

Table 4-1   *crontab* Items

crontab Entry	Range
Minute at which to execute	0-59
Hour at which to execute	0-23 (Midnight is 0.)
Day of the month on which to execute	1-31
Month of the year on which to execute	1-12
Day of the week on which to execute	0-6 (Sunday is 0.)
Command to execute	(Enter the command.)

The *crontab* file is a text file that can be created through any text editor such as vi. The only requirement is that the file must be called *crontab*. Here are some examples of entries that could go in a *crontab* file.

- To display a long listing of your directory at noon on the first day of each month, you would enter the following (the asterisks tell UNIX to include all values):

```
0 12 1 * * ls -l
```

- To print a file called *myjunk* to a printer queue named *Print1* at 9:00 p.m. on each Thursday, you would enter:

```
0 21 * * 4 lpr -PPrint1 myjunk
```

- To copy a file called *report1* from the */etc* directory to your home directory (~) on the 15th of each month at 8:35 a.m., you would enter:

```
35 8 15 * * cp /etc/report1 ~
```

All these commands can be lumped into one *crontab* file that you can set up in your home directory and forget about. The UNIX system will be responsible for the scheduling and running of the commands in the *crontab* file.

4-5   LIVING WITHIN YOUR QUOTA

Many schools limit the amount of disk space a student can use. The reason for this is simple: Disk space is still somewhat expensive, and many students tend to keep everything they ever put in their account. If you find that you are running low on available disk space, this section will assist you in compacting your files.

Stuffing Many Files into One: tar

tar stands for tape archive, which was the original use for the command. If you wanted to back up sections of your UNIX computer onto tape, you would create a tape archive. How does this help with your disk quota problems? It's a lot easier to work with one big file than many little ones. Which would you rather copy to a disk: 1 file or 100 files?

Let's say that I want to convert the contents of my *robo* directory into one big file. Here's what's in my *robo* directory.

```
zard:~$ cd robo
zard:~/robo$ ls
BACK.GIF      END           MENUICON.GIF   TESTICON.GIF   robo3.htm
CIM.GIF       HOMEICON.GIF  NEXTICON.GIF   UPICON.GIF     robo4.htm
CMNTICON.GIF  IMSE.GIF      PREVICON.GIF   contents.htm   robo5.htm
CNTSICON.GIF  INDXICON.GIF  SRCHICON.GIF   robo1.htm      robo6.htm
DOWNICON.GIF  MAINICON.GIF  SWASH5.GIF     robo2.htm      title.htm
zard:~/robo$
```

To convert all this into one file, I use the tar command with the following option: -cf, which tells UNIX to create a tar file with the name following the f. (I'm going to call mine *robotar*.) All I need to do then is specify what files I want placed in the tar file, which is everything, so I use an asterisk (*).

```
zard:~/robo$ tar -cf robotar *
zard:~/robo$ ls -l robotar
-rw-r--r--   1 sjames   users       102400 Sep  5 11:55 robotar
zard:~/robo$
```

The tar file was created. To see what's in it, I will use the tar -tvf command. The t stands for test, v stands for verbose listing, and f specifies the filename.

```
zard:~/robo$ tar -tvf robotar
-rw-rw-r-- sjames/users    4247 Mar  7 09:40 1996 BACK.GIF
-rw-rw-r-- sjames/users    1439 Mar  7 09:40 1996 CIM.GIF
-rw-rw-r-- sjames/users    1394 Mar  7 09:40 1996 CMNTICON.GIF
-rw-rw-r-- sjames/users    1468 Mar  7 09:40 1996 CNTSICON.GIF
-rw-rw-r-- sjames/users    1161 Mar  7 09:40 1996 DOWNICON.GIF
-rw-rw-r-- sjames/users      71 Mar  7 09:40 1996 END
-rw-rw-r-- sjames/users    1239 Mar  7 09:40 1996 HOMEICON.GIF
-rw-rw-r-- sjames/users   38037 Mar  7 09:40 1996 IMSE.GIF
-rw-rw-r-- sjames/users    1543 Mar  7 09:40 1996 INDXICON.GIF
-rw-rw-r-- sjames/users    1198 Mar  7 09:40 1996 MAINICON.GIF
-rw-rw-r-- sjames/users    1183 Mar  7 09:40 1996 MENUICON.GIF
-rw-rw-r-- sjames/users    1232 Mar  7 09:40 1996 NEXTICON.GIF
-rw-rw-r-- sjames/users    1221 Mar  7 09:40 1996 PREVICON.GIF
-rw-rw-r-- sjames/users    1497 Mar  7 09:40 1996 SRCHICON.GIF
-rw-rw-r-- sjames/users    2504 Mar  7 09:40 1996 SWASH5.GIF
-rw-rw-r-- sjames/users    1223 Mar  7 09:40 1996 TESTICON.GIF
-rw-rw-r-- sjames/users    1222 Mar  7 09:40 1996 UPICON.GIF
-rw-rw-r-- sjames/users     906 Mar  7 09:40 1996 contents.htm
-rw-rw-r-- sjames/users    1223 Mar  7 09:40 1996 robo1.htm
-rw-rw-r-- sjames/users    1501 Mar  7 09:40 1996 robo2.htm
-rw-rw-r-- sjames/users    2051 Mar  7 09:40 1996 robo3.htm
-rw-rw-r-- sjames/users    1377 Mar  7 09:40 1996 robo4.htm
```

```
-rw-rw-r-- sjames/users   1345 Mar  7 09:40 1996 robo5.htm
-rw-rw-r-- sjames/users   1392 Mar  7 09:40 1996 robo6.htm
-rw-rw-r-- sjames/users    903 Mar  7 09:40 1996 title.htm
zard:~/robo$
```

I now have one big file instead of many little ones. I can then copy this file to a disk or store it someplace else. When I'm ready, I can pull all the files back out of it with the tar -xvf command, which says to extract (x), in verbose mode (v), everything that is in the filename supplied after the f. Verbose mode simply means make tar show what it's doing. I'll now create a new directory, copy the *robotar* file there, and extract the files from it.

```
zard:~/robo$ mkdir robot
zard:~/robo$ cd robot
zard:~/robo/robot$ cp ../robotar .
zard:~/robo/robot$ tar -xvf robotar
BACK.GIF
CIM.GIF
CMNTICON.GIF
CNTSICON.GIF
DOWNICON.GIF
END
HOMEICON.GIF
IMSE.GIF
INDXICON.GIF
MAINICON.GIF
MENUICON.GIF
NEXTICON.GIF
PREVICON.GIF
SRCHICON.GIF
SWASH5.GIF
TESTICON.GIF
UPICON.GIF
contents.htm
robo1.htm
robo2.htm
robo3.htm
robo4.htm
robo5.htm
robo6.htm
title.htm
zard:~/robo/robot$
```

I have successfully restored all the files from the tar file.

Putting the Squeeze on Your Files: compress and uncompress

In the last example, you saw how to place many files into a single file. The primary reason you did this was so that you had to deal with only one file. However, this procedure did nothing to help your quota dilemma since the tar file is simply the sum of all the little files. The *compress* command will squeeze a file down, making it much smaller than the original. If you can do this on various big files that are eating up a lot of room in your directories, you can get some breathing space within your quota.

The syntax of the `compress` command is `compress` *filetocompress*. You should use the `compress` command after you have placed files into an archive with the `tar` command. I will apply this command to my *robotar* file.

```
zard:~/robo/robot$ compress robotar
zard:~/robo/robot$ ls -l
total 85
-rw-r--r--   1 sjames    users         85021 Sep  5 12:13 robotar.Z
zard:~/robo/robot$
```

There's the compressed version of the file. Notice that the `.Z` extension has been placed at the end of the filename. That's how you can tell that a file has been compressed. Let's take a peek at how big the original version was.

```
zard:~/robo/robot$ ls -l ../robotar
-rw-r--r--   1 sjames    users        102400 Sep  5 11:55 ../robotar
zard:~/robo/robot$
```

The original was 102,400 bytes, whereas the compressed version of the file is only 85,021. I saved 17,379 bytes, or about 17 percent off the original file size. That figure isn't too bad, considering the **tar** file contained some binary image files that probably couldn't be compressed a lot.

Several different compression techniques are available. Most compression algorithms work by replacing recurring patterns of data with a single code that is stored in a table. For example, if I were to replace the word *UNIX* with the code *U*, I would save three characters for every occurrence of the word *UNIX*.

The uncompression algorithms work in the opposite direction of the compression algorithms. Each code in the compressed file is replaced with its original value from the code table. In other words, the single *U* code would be replaced with the full *UNIX* value.

If you run across a compressed file, you must *uncompress* it before you can do anything with it. The command for this is `uncompress` *filename*.

```
zard:~/robo/robot$ uncompress robotar.Z
zard:~/robo/robot$ ls -l
total 101
-rw-r--r--   1 sjames    users        102400 Sep  5 12:13 robotar
zard:~/robo/robot$
```

I now have my original **tar** file back. Remember that you need to extract the files from the **tar** file before you can do anything useful with them.

Another File Compression Command: `gzip`

gzip is not a standard UNIX command, but you should know about it since most UNIX system administrators are putting copies of it on their systems. `gzip` is used in the same manner as `compress`; that is, it squeezes files down. I mention `gzip` because it often does a better job than `compress`, and `gzip` is a very common format for compressed files. `gzip` files end with a *.gz* or *.gzip* extension.

I will compress the `tar` file once again, except this time I will use `gzip`.

```
zard:~/robo$ tar -cf robotar *
zard:~/robo$ ls -l robotar
-rw-r--r--  1 sjames   users       102400 Sep  5 14:24 robotar
zard:~/robo$ gzip robotar
zard:~/robo$ ls -l robotar.gz
-rw-r--r--  1 sjames   users        56023 Sep  5 14:24 robotar.gz
zard:~/robo$
```

You can see that the *robotar.gz* file is almost 50 percent smaller than the original *robotar* `tar` file. The command `gzip` *robotar* was responsible for compressing the file and then renaming the file with a *.gz* extension.

Before you can use what's stored in a `gzip` file, you must decompress the files. This is done via the `gzip -d` command.

```
zard:~/robo$ mkdir robot2
zard:~/robo$ cd robot2
zard:~/robo/robot2$ cp ../robotar.gz .
zard:~/robo/robot2$ ls -l
total 56
-rw-r--r--  1 sjames   users        56023 Sep  5 14:29 robotar.gz
zard:~/robo/robot2$ gzip -d robotar.gz
zard:~/robo/robot2$ ls -l
total 91
-rw-r--r--  1 sjames   users       102400 Sep  5 14:29 robotar
zard:~/robo/robot2$
```

You can see that the `gzip -d` command worked, and the original `tar` file is back. Remember that you still need to extract the `tar` files before they can be used.

4-6 OTHER UNIX COMMANDS

This section is simply a collection of other UNIX commands that you may find useful. The commands are listed alphabetically by command name.

Displaying a Basic Calculator: bc

If you don't have a calculator handy, but you are logged onto your UNIX host, you might find *bc* to be useful. bc lets you use the standard four operators (+, −, *, /), just like on a normal calculator. To stop bc, press (CTRL)-**D**. Let's take a look at bc.

```
zard:~$ bc
bc 1.02 (Mar 3, 92) Copyright (C) 1991, 1992 Free Software Foundation, Inc.
This is free software with ABSOLUTELY NO WARRANTY.
For details type `warranty'.
4 * 5
20
1 + 2 + 3
6
```

```
15 - 6 * 30
-165
(15 - 6) * 30
270
[stopped]
zard:~$
```

Try It

Use bc to compute the following problems. (Remember you must press CTRL-**D** to stop bc.)

1. (48 – 12) / 3

2. 10 * 408

3. 32 – (12 / 4)

4. (18 * 5) + 105

Displaying a Calendar: cal

The *cal* command will print out a monthly or yearly calendar. To get a calendar of the current month, simply type **cal**.

```
zard:~$ cal
    September 1996
 S  M Tu  W Th  F  S
 1  2  3  4  5  6  7
 8  9 10 11 12 13 14
15 16 17 18 19 20 21
22 23 24 25 26 27 28
29 30

zard:~$
```

To get a calendar of the year, enter **cal 1996**.

```
zard:~$ cal 1996
                         1996

       January              February              March
 S  M Tu  W Th  F  S   S  M Tu  W Th  F  S   S  M Tu  W Th  F  S
    1  2  3  4  5  6            1  2  3               1  2
 7  8  9 10 11 12 13   4  5  6  7  8  9 10   3  4  5  6  7  8  9
14 15 16 17 18 19 20  11 12 13 14 15 16 17  10 11 12 13 14 15 16
21 22 23 24 25 26 27  18 19 20 21 22 23 24  17 18 19 20 21 22 23
28 29 30 31           25 26 27 28 29        24 25 26 27 28 29 30
                                            31

        April                 May                  June
 S  M Tu  W Th  F  S   S  M Tu  W Th  F  S   S  M Tu  W Th  F  S
    1  2  3  4  5  6            1  2  3  4                     1
 7  8  9 10 11 12 13   5  6  7  8  9 10 11   2  3  4  5  6  7  8
14 15 16 17 18 19 20  12 13 14 15 16 17 18   9 10 11 12 13 14 15
21 22 23 24 25 26 27  19 20 21 22 23 24 25  16 17 18 19 20 21 22
28 29 30              26 27 28 29 30 31      23 24 25 26 27 28 29
                                             30
```

```
         July                    August                  September
 S  M Tu  W Th  F  S      S  M Tu  W Th  F  S      S  M Tu  W Th  F  S
    1  2  3  4  5  6               1  2  3      1  2  3  4  5  6  7
 7  8  9 10 11 12 13      4  5  6  7  8  9 10      8  9 10 11 12 13 14
14 15 16 17 18 19 20     11 12 13 14 15 16 17     15 16 17 18 19 20 21
21 22 23 24 25 26 27     18 19 20 21 22 23 24     22 23 24 25 26 27 28
28 29 30 31             25 26 27 28 29 30 31     29 30

        October                 November                 December
 S  M Tu  W Th  F  S      S  M Tu  W Th  F  S      S  M Tu  W Th  F  S
       1  2  3  4  5               1  2      1  2  3  4  5  6  7
 6  7  8  9 10 11 12      3  4  5  6  7  8  9      8  9 10 11 12 13 14
13 14 15 16 17 18 19     10 11 12 13 14 15 16     15 16 17 18 19 20 21
20 21 22 23 24 25 26     17 18 19 20 21 22 23     22 23 24 25 26 27 28
27 28 29 30 31           24 25 26 27 28 29 30     29 30 31

zard:~$
```

Try It

Use the `cal` command to print the calendar for September 1752. Why does the month look so weird? (You'll need to do some historical research.) The command is **cal 9 1752** ⏎.

Clearing Your Screen: `clear`

The *clear* command does what it says: It clears your screen.

Finding the Differences Between Two Files: `diff`

The *diff* command compares two files and reports on any differences between them. The command format is `diff` *file1 file2*. Assume that you have the following files:

Contents of *oldfile*:

```
This is a file
this file looks very close to the other file
but there are some very minor changes.
In 1814, there were over 4000 in America
and the numbers keep growing
where will
they stop?
```

Contents of *newfile*:

```
This is a file
actually another file
this file looks very close to the other file
but there are some very minor changes.
In 1817, there were over 4000 in America
and the numbers keep growing
where will
they stop?
Who knows
```

See what `diff` tells you about the differences between the two files.

```
zard:~$ diff oldfile newfile
1a2
> actually another file
4c5
< In 1814, there were over 4000 in America
---
> In 1817, there were over 4000 in America
7c8,9
< they stop?
---
> they stop?
> Who knows
```

Any line that starts with a < indicates that line is in the first file (*oldfile*). A > indicates that the line is in the second file (*newfile*). The numbers and letters indicate what differences were encountered. The 1a2 indicates that a line was *added* between lines 1 and 2. The 4c5 indicates that there was a *change* between line 4 in the first file and line 5 in the second file. This makes sense since the date in that line was changed. The 7c8,9 indicates there was a change between line 7 of the first file and lines 8 and 9 of the second file, which is correct since a line was added. (Some versions of diff correctly catch the addition of the last line as an a, whereas others see it as a c.) The only other letter you might encounter from diff would be a d for delete.

Try It

Try out the diff command in this Try It!

1. Create the following file in a text editor and call it *version1*:

```
The grass is green,
the dirt is brown,
just what's in the air all around?
```

2. Create the following file in a text editor and call it *version2*:

```
The grass is GREEN
old dirt is brown,
there's a smell,
just what's in the air all around?
```

3. Now use the diff command to locate the differences in the files.

```
diff version1 version2 ⏎
```

4. Examine the reported differences and see if you agree with them.

Printing Messages to the Screen: echo

The *echo* command simply writes the message that you give it to the screen. Table 4-2 lists some of the special characters that can be embedded in the message that you want to send to the screen.

Table 4-2   Special Characters for the echo Command

Character	Purpose
\b	Inserts a backspace character
\c	Prevents echo from skipping a line after it prints the message out
\n	Inserts a newline character (has the same effect as skipping a line)
\t	Inserts a tab character
\\	Inserts a backslash (\) character

Here are some examples of the echo command.

```
zard:~$ echo "Hello there"
Hello there
zard:~$ echo "This is\nnot too bad"
This is
not too bad
zard:~$ echo "Not a problem\\"
Not a problem\
zard:~$
```

Locating Files on the Computer: find

The *find* command does just what it says: It finds files. Once find locates a file, you can have the command perform some action on the located file(s). The basic syntax of the command is find *where-to-look what-to-look-for action-to-perform*. Let's find any files in my home directory that start with the letter *n*.

```
zard:~$ find /home/sjames -name "n*" -print
/home/sjames/newfile
/home/sjames/newfile~
zard:~$
```

Two files were returned. The find command was told to start looking in my home directory and any directories underneath it. The command was to look for files whose names started with *n*. The action to carry out upon finding any matching files was simply to print the name of those files.

Names are not the only criteria that you can use to select files. Let's find any files in my home directory that were not modified in ten days or more. I'm not going to show the output of all these variations of find since they would eat up a lot of space.

```
find /home/sjames -mtime +10 -print
```

That -mtime portion of the command means modification time. The +10 means files modified more than ten days ago (-10 would mean files modified *less* than ten days ago). Again, the requested action is simply to print the filenames.

If I wanted to locate all files on the system owned by me (at least where I have permission to look), I would enter the following command:

```
find / -user sjames -print
```

This version of the command tells find to look in the root directory (/) and everything underneath it for any files owned by user *sjames*. If any files are located, UNIX should simply print the filenames.

Here is an example where the action is something other than printing:

```
find /home/sjames -name "*.tmp" -exec rm { } \;
```

This command tells find to locate any files ending in *.tmp* under my home directory. The action of this find command is not to print the names, but rather to delete the files that are found by the command. The -exec option indicates that the action is to execute a command, rm. The braces { } indicate where the filename should appear in the rm command. The \; characters are a find requirement to end the -exec action.

You should consult the man page for find to learn of other options that can be used to locate files.

Try It Use the find command in this Try It! to locate any files in (or under) the */etc* directory that start with *h*. Have the command simply print the filenames. The command is find /etc -name "h*" -print.

Searching for a Phrase in a File: grep

Sometimes you just can't remember which file contains some text that you are looking for. The *grep* command, or global regular expression parser, will look through the text files that you specify and report whether or not that file contains the text that you are looking for. The basic syntax of the command is grep *phrase files*. Let's see if I have any files that contain the word *America*.

```
zard:~$ grep "America" *
grep: Mail: Is a directory
internetwork-mail-guide:#N aol; America Online; America Online, Inc.;
newfile:In 1817, there were over 4000 in America
newfile~:In 1814, there were over 4000 in America
oldfile:In 1814, there were over 4000 in America
grep: public_html: Is a directory
grep: robo: Is a directory
grep: temp: Is a directory
zard:~$
```

You can see that any directories were skipped, which means that the remaining lines are files where the word *america* was found along with the actual line from the file.

Take a look at the next example, which doesn't find the word *america*.

```
zard:~$ grep "america" *
grep: Mail: Is a directory
grep: public_html: Is a directory
grep: robo: Is a directory
grep: temp: Is a directory
zard:~$
```

Why didn't this command find *america*? Remember that UNIX is case sensitive, and so is the `grep` command. There are instances of the word *America* but not *america*. You can add a `-i` to the command to tell it to ignore case sensitivity.

```
zard:~$ grep -i "america" *
grep: Mail: Is a directory
internetwork-mail-guide:#N aol; America Online; America Online, Inc.;
newfile:In 1817, there were over 4000 in America
newfile~:In 1814, there were over 4000 in America
oldfile:In 1814, there were over 4000 in America
grep: public_html: Is a directory
grep: robo: Is a directory
grep: temp: Is a directory
zard:~$
```

The original results are again displayed.

Keeping People from Bothering You: mesg

If you're busy at work, it can be annoying to have people trying to talk to you via the `talk` command. If you would like to stop being bothered, use the *mesg* command. `mesg` comes in two flavors: `mesg y` (which means you want messages) or `mesg n` (which means you don't want messages).

Suppose I enter the following:

```
zard:~$ mesg n
zard:~$
```

Now if anyone tries to talk to me, that user will see the following message: `Your party is refusing messages`. This command will also effectively stop the `write` command.

Sorting Files: sort

The *sort* command alphabetically arranges the contents of a file. The syntax of the `sort` command is `sort filename`. If you want the sorted results to go someplace else, use `sort filename -o outputfilename`. This version of the command alphabetizes the contents of *filename* and places that sorted information in another file called *outputfile*.

Assume that I have the following text in the file called *compbrand*:

```
Packard Bell
Acer
AT&T
Compaq
IBM
Sun
Silicon Graphics
DEC
```

If I want to sort the file and have the sorted version stuck right back into the *compbrand* file, I use the following command:

```
zard:~$ sort compbrand
zard:~$ more compbrand
AT&T
Acer
Compaq
DEC
IBM
Packard Bell
Silicon Graphics
Sun
zard:~$
```

If I want the sorted version to appear in a different file, I need to add the -o option to the end of the command.

```
zard:~$ sort compbrand -o sorted
zard:~$ more sorted
AT&T
Acer
Compaq
DEC
IBM
Packard Bell
Silicon Graphics
Sun
zard:~$
```

Try It   Try sorting the contents of a file.

1. Type the following list in any text editor, and save it in a file named *tosort*.

   banana
   orange
   grapes
   apple
   plum

2. Sort the file, and place the sorted version back into the original file.

   sort tosort↵

Writing a Message to Another User's Screen: `write`

The *write* command allows you to send a message to another user who is currently logged on to the system and has not disabled messages (no `mesg n`). The syntax for the command is `write` *user*. After you have issued the command, you can start typing your message. When you are finished with the message, press (CTRL)-**D** to stop the `write` command.

I will send a message to user *vjames*:

```
zard:~$ write vjames
Hello there
The printer needs paper, please.
zard:~$
```

When I finish typing, I press (CTRL)-**D** to stop the `write` command.

User *vjames,* who has not disabled messaging with the `mesg` command, sees the following on her screen.

```
zard:~$
Message from sjames@zard on ttyp0 at 11:32 …
Hello there!
The printer needs paper, please.
zard:~$
```

4-7 WRITING SHELL SCRIPTS

You've now looked at many of the different commands that are available under the UNIX system. The last item that you will learn how to write is a shell script. A *shell script* is a set of commands that you want executed by the shell (remember from Chapter 1 that the shell is your interface to the computer). It's very similar to recording a series of commands that you type on the keyboard and then having the computer play them back. Shell scripts are called batch files on other computer systems.

Shell scripts are very powerful entities. In fact, far more can be done with them than will be shown in this section. An entire programming language can be placed within a shell script to allow the shell script to make a decision and then act upon the outcome of that decision. There are also looping controls that will allow the shell script to repeat certain commands a given number of times or until some event happens. This book was not designed to be a tutorial on programming concepts, nor does it make any assumptions about your programming background. Therefore, you will not be examining any of the shell script programming constructs.

Shell scripts are created much the same way as Fortran or C programs. A standard text editor is used to type in the commands that you want executed. The main difference between shell scripts and programming language programs is that shell scripts do not get compiled. Shell scripts are interpreted, which means the computer looks at a line, executes that line, and then fetches the next line. Consequently, shell scripts are somewhat slower than compiled programs but are generally easier to maintain.

To see how shell scripts work, let's write a shell script that reports the system date and who is doing what on the system. First I need to start my text editor, vi. I then enter the following commands into my file, just as I usually do when typing them from the keyboard:

```
date
w
```

Then I save the file. I'm going to save it with the name *checkout*.

Next I need to change the permissions of the file so that it is marked as an *executable file*. All shell scripts must have the execute permission set on. I use the chmod command to change the permissions:

```
zard:~$ chmod 700 checkout
zard:~$ ls -l checkout
-rwx------   1 sjames    users          7 Sep  9 11:42 checkout*
zard:~$
```

The program has the execute permission set. Now, I'll run the program.

```
zard:~$ checkout
Mon Sep  9 11:46:15 EDT 1996
 11:46am  up 8 days, 10:41,  2 users,  load average: 0.00, 0.00, 0.00
User     tty      from             login@ idle  JCPU  PCPU what
sjames   ttyp0    192.138.137.203 11:42am                  -bash
vjames   tty1                     11:46am                  -bash
zard:~$
```

In addition to having created a shell script that I can run anytime, I can use other UNIX concepts, such as redirection, with the shell script. For example, I can send a copy of the output of the shell script to a file.

```
zard:~$ checkout > mycheckout.dat
zard:~$
```

To make sure the file is there, I use ls.

```
zard:~$ ls -l mycheckout.dat
-rw-r--r--   1 sjames    users        305 Sep  9 11:47 mycheckout.dat
zard:~$
```

Now that I have the output redirected to a file, I can look at it with the more command or I can print it. Here's what's in the file.

```
zard:~$ more mycheckout.dat
Mon Sep  9 11:47:15 EDT 1996
 11:47am  up 8 days, 10:42,  2 users,  load average: 0.00, 0.00, 0.00
User     tty      from             login@ idle  JCPU  PCPU what
sjames   ttyp0    192.138.137.203 11:42am                  -bash
vjames   tty1                     11:46am        1         -bash
zard:~$
```

I can also add `echo` lines to the shell script to provide a little bit more information to myself or other users of the script. I will change the last shell script a little bit so that it tells what's going on. Here's what the revised *checkout* shell script should look like.

```
echo "Today is"
date
echo "\n"
echo "Here's who is on the system and what they're up to…\n"
w
```

This is what the output of the modified shell script looks like.

```
zard:~$ checkout
Today is
Mon Sep  9 11:50:50 EDT 1996

Here's who is on the system and what they're up to...
 11:50am  up 8 days, 10:46,  2 users,  load average: 0.00, 0.00, 0.00
User     tty      from              login@ idle  JCPU   PCPU  what
sjames   ttyp0    192.138.137.203 11:42am         1            -bash
vjames   tty1                     11:46am   4                  -bash
zard:~$
```

If you want to, you can add comments to your shell scripts. The comments aren't executed by the UNIX computer; they are just there to provide some information that you want tagged along with your shell script. Let's add some comments to the preceding shell script and make another change so that the script looks to see if user *vjames* is logged on to the system. All shell script comments start with #.

```
# Checkout shell script
#
#  Written by Scott James
echo "Today is"
date
echo "\n"
echo "Here's who is on the system and what they're up to…\n"
w
# Let's find out if user vjames is on the system
echo "\n"
echo "Is vjames around?"
w | grep "vjames"
```

When I execute this shell script, it will print the current date and time, who is on the system, and what each user is doing, and it will specifically look for user *vjames* showing up in the w command. Let's take a look at this.

```
zard:~$ checkout
Today is
Mon Sep  9 11:54:03 EDT 1996

Here's who is on the system and what they're up to...
 11:54am  up 8 days, 10:49,  2 users,  load average: 0.00, 0.00, 0.00
User     tty      from             login@ idle  JCPU  PCPU  what
sjames   ttyp0    192.138.137.203 11:42am          1            -bash
vjames   tty1                     11:46am    7                  -bash
larnold  tty2     itso.det1.com   11:48am                       -bash

Is vjames around?
vjames   tty1                     11:46am    7                  -bash
zard:~$
```

You can see that the shell script acts just as before, with the addition that the script now reports on user *vjames* separately.

Using Variables in Shell Programs

The concept of a variable isn't difficult to understand. A *variable* is a place where you can store some data and change that data if you like. You can add variables to your shell scripts that will allow you to have the user interact with the shell script and supply it information. A secondary use for variables in shell scripts is to define items that may change over time. For example, the following creates a shell script with a variable that stores a printer's name:

```
ptr="HPLaserPrinter1"
lpr -P$ptr myfile
lpr -P$ptr myfile2
lpr -P$ptr myfile 3
```

Why would I want to do this? Look at the typing that I have saved myself by defining the variable and then using the variable in the `lpr` lines. The `ptr=HPLaserPrinter1` line is where I actually created the variable and then assigned a value to the variable. I put double quotation marks around the printer's name to make sure that the shell script evaluates it correctly. Any time there is a possibility that there could be spaces or special characters in a variable's value, you need to enclose that variable's value in double quotation marks. `$ptr` tells the shell script that it should substitute the variable's value at that point.

The second reason I might want to put the printer's name into a variable is that the printer's name might change in the future. Rather than altering three lines in my script, I need to change only one: the line where I actually plugged the printer's name into the variable `ptr`.

You can also let the user type information into a variable inside a shell script. This is carried out through the `read` command, which is available in most UNIX shells. Let's write a shell script called *easyfind*, which prompts the shell script user for the pieces of information that the `find` command needs. Here's what the *easyfind* script looks like.

```
echo "Where should I start searching from?"
read location
echo "What is the name of the file that I should look for?"
read filename
echo "I will begin the search!"
find $location -name "$filename" -print
echo "The search is over!"
```

Notice that the first thing that the shell script does is prompt the user for the directory where he or she wants to search from. Whatever the user types goes into the variable named *location*. The shell script then prompts the user for the filename that the user wants to look for. This information is stored in the variable called *filename*. The shell script then starts the `find` command. Notice that `$filename` was enclosed in double quotation marks on the `find` line to ensure that it is handled correctly if there are any special characters. Don't forget to change the script's mode with `chmod` so that it is executable.

Let's take a look at this script in action.

```
zard:~$ chmod 700 easyfind
zard:~$ ls -l easyfind
-rwx------   1 sjames    users       231 Sep  9 12:27 easyfind*
zard:~$ easyfind
Where should I start searching from?
/home/sjames
What is the name of the file that I should look for?
myche*
I will begin the search!
/home/sjames/mycheckout.dat
The search is over!
zard:~$
```

Working with Command-Line Parameters

So far you have worked with UNIX commands that take information right from the command line. For example, when I typed **telnet nova.gmi.edu**, the computer used the information following the `telnet` command as the address of the computer that I wanted to connect to. Information supplied on the same line as the command and then interpreted as input to the command is known as a *command-line parameter*. Command-line parameters are easy to work with in shell scripts. Each piece of information on the command line is simply numbered sequentially in the shell script. The first piece is $1, the second piece is $2, and so on. Pieces of information are separated by spaces. Therefore, if you are typing something that contains spaces on the command line, and you want it interpreted as one item, enclose the item in double quotation marks.

Let's rewrite the last shell script example, *easyfind*, so that it uses command-line parameters.

```
echo "I will begin the search!"
find $1 -name "$2" -print
echo "The search is over!"
```

This version of the shell script works the same way as the previous version with the exception that the user must provide the two pieces of information on the command line. Here's the same search executed with the revised shell script.

```
zard:~$ easyfind /home/sjames myche*
I will begin the search!
/home/sjames/mycheckout.dat
The search is over!
zard:~$
```

Notice what happens if the user doesn't supply all the pieces of information.

```
zard:~$ easyfind
I will begin the search!
The search is over!
zard:~$
```

The only results of the shell script are the echo lines. Since there wasn't enough information for the find command to work, it never executed. This is the point where programming skills come in handy since you could revise the script to make sure that the two pieces of information are supplied. As stated before, programming constructs are available that could check for the required two pieces of information. If both pieces were not supplied, you could have the shell script generate an error message. Only if everything was supplied would the shell script execute. It is beyond the scope of this book to discuss these issues. You should refer to one of the operating systems manuals for your UNIX computer for more information on shell script programming.

SUMMARY

This chapter examined some of the more advanced UNIX operations that you should be aware of. You learned about programming language compilers under UNIX and how to run multiple processes in the foreground and background. You learned how to monitor and change process priorities and how to get UNIX to run processes at specific times. You also learned how to squeeze files down by using some of the UNIX commands. This chapter also presented many additional UNIX commands that are useful to know. The chapter concluded with an examination of shell scripts.

At this point, you should be familiar with most of the basics of the UNIX operating system. As with most tools, the more you use UNIX, the better you will become with it. Good luck!

Key Words

at	grep
Background	gzip
bc	jobs
bg	kill
C	mesg
cal	nice
cc	Object program
clear	Pascal
Command-line parameters	Priority
Compilers	Programming languages
compress	ps
cron	Shell scripts
date	sort
diff	Source program
echo	System load average
Executable files	tar
f77	uncompress
fg	uptime
find	Variables
Foreground	write
Fortran	

Exercises

1. Type the following program in a text editor. Save the file as *ex1.c*.

    ```
    #include <stdio.h>

    main()
    {
      int num;

      printf("Enter a whole number\n");
      scanf("%d",&num);
      printf("Your number, %d, squared is %d.\n",num,num*num);
    }
    ```

    Compile the program with `cc`. If there are any errors, fix them. When the program compiles correctly, run it. Print the source file.

2. Execute the `ps` command. Write down each line, and explain what each line is for. Explain how you would stop one of the processes running with the `kill` command, and write down the exact command that you would type into the computer.

3. Redirect the system load information to a file. Print that file.

4. Write down how you would get the computer to print a file called *tech.dat* in exactly five minutes from now. Specify which commands you would use to do this.

5. Write down the *crontab* file entries for the following:
    a. Display a directory listing of the entire system every Monday.
    b. Print the file called *rfdata.dat* at 5 p.m. on the 20th of each month.
    c. Copy the file */usr/bin/report5* to ~ at noon on the first of each month.

6. Use bc to calculate the following:
    a. 50 * 4096 / 32
    b. 108.5 – (30 * 4.6)
    c. –405 * (–504 / (12 * 15.4))

7. Redirect a copy of the calendar for the current year to a file. Print that file.

8. Create *file1* with the following lines:

```
Here is the time
for all people to
come to the aid
of their computer.
```

  Create *file2* with the following lines:

```
Here is the time
FOR all people to
ever
come to the aid
of his/her computer.
```

  Run the diff command, and redirect the results to a file. Print the redirected file, and explain what each line in the file means.

9. Use the find command to locate all files in the */etc* directory that starts with the letter *i*. Write down how many files the command returned. (If the list is long, you might have to pipe it through more.)

10. Create a text file called *needtosort*. Put the following entries in the file:

```
dog
cat
elephant
ant
frog
otter
snake
turtle
lynx
whale
giraffe
```

  Sort the file, and place the output of the sort command in a file called *thisissorted*. Print both files, and write the command that you used to perform the sort on the bottom of the unsorted file printout.

11. Send a message to a friend via the write command. Make sure that you both have enabled mesg y. Send a write command to your friend. Then have your friend disable messaging. Send another write command to your friend. Write a paragraph describing your experience.

12. Create a shell script called *mydir* that prints a long listing of your directory. Print the shell script.

13. Modify the shell script *mydir* so that it uses command-line parameters to get the directory name. Print the shell script.

14. Write a shell script that allows the user to specify files to look in and a phrase to look for; that is, create a friendly version of the grep command. Print the shell script.

Appendix A: More on Text Editors

The purpose of this appendix is to provide you with more information on using text editors under UNIX. In particular, it explores a few of the advanced functions in *vi* and the following editors: *joe*, *pico*, and **emacs**. This section is not meant to be an all-inclusive listing of the capabilities of each editor; rather, it is designed to serve as a quick reference to command shortcuts.

vi

You have previously examined many of the basic functions of the *vi* editor. This section concentrates on other common functions. Each of the various command sections will be presented in a table format showing the available commands.

Searching for Text
To search for text within *vi*, type : to make sure that you are in last-line mode.

vi Command	What It Does
/ text	Searches forward through the file for the text that you specify
/ ? text	Searches backward through the file for the text that you specify
n	Finds the next occurrence of the text if one exists

After the search is over, you are placed back in *vi*'s command mode.

Deleting Text
These text deletion commands work from the *vi* command mode.

vi Command	What It Does
x	Deletes a character
dw	Deletes a word
dd	Deletes a line
dG	Deletes from the cursor location to the end of the file
d0	Deletes from the cursor location to the start of the file
D or d$	Deletes from the cursor location to the end of the line

Moving Text
Before attempting to move text, type : to make sure that you are in last-line mode. Then turn line numbering on by typing **set nu**. To move text, specify the starting line number of the block to move, the ending line number of the block to move, and the target location of the move in the following format: startline#, endline#, targetline#. The text is moved to the line below targetline#. If you want to undo a move operation, press u.

Changing Text
The text-changing commands work from the command mode and place you into the input mode of *vi*. Place the cursor at the beginning of the word or line that you want to change.

vi Command	What It Does
cw	Changes a single word
#cw	Changes a specified number of words
C	Changes text to the end of the line
&	Marks the end of the line currently being edited
xp	Corrects transposed characters

Replacing Text
The text replacement commands operate from the editor's command mode. Position the cursor at the beginning of the line or on the character that is to be replaced.

vi Command	What It Does
r	Replaces a single character and immediately returns you to command mode
R	Replaces text until (ESC) is pressed

joe

joe is an extremely easy-to-use text editor that allows you to move around with the cursor keys and make corrections with the (BACKSPACE) key. Many users find *joe* much easier to use than *vi* since *joe* is quite similar in function to most word processors. In fact, there are only three keystrokes that a *joe* user must absolutely know about.

Joe Keystroke	What It Does
(CTRL)-K H	Brings up the help system
(CTRL)-K X	Saves the file being edited in joe and then exits the editor
(CTRL)-C	Quits joe, losing any changes that were made

joe is usually started with the filename to be edited placed after the command name. Just as in *vi*, if the file already exists, it will be opened in the editor. If the file does not exist, it will be created. Let's take a look at starting *joe*:

```
zard:~$ joe test.dat

test.dat                        Ctrl-K H for help
New File


  :

** Joe's Own Editor v1.0.6 ** Copyright (C)1992 Joseph H. Allen **
```

At this point, you are in the editor and can start typing whatever you want. The third line of the screen tells you that *test.dat* is a new file. You should also notice that the screen always provides some navigation tools to help you move around inside the editor.

Let's take a look at getting some help by pressing (CTRL)-**K H**:

```
test.dat                        Ctrl-K H for help


  :

Basic   Windows   Advanced Options   Search   Names   Joe
```

joe's help system allows you to choose from several different areas that you might want help on. Let's just take a look at basic help:

```
Help Screen    turn off with ^KH
CURSOR          GO TO           BLOCK     DELETE  MISC      EXIT
^B left ^F right ^U  prev. screen ^KB begin ^D char. ^KJ reformat ^KX save
^P up   ^N down  ^V  next screen  ^KK end   ^Y line  ^TT overtype ^C abort
^Z previous word ^A beg. of line ^KM move   ^W >word ` Ctrl-    ^KZ shell
^X next word    ^E  end of line  ^KC copy  ^O word< ^\ Meta-    FILE
SEARCH          ^KU top of file  ^KW file  ^J >line ^R retype  ^KE new
^KF find text   ^KV end of file  ^KY delete ^_ undo ^@ insert  ^KR insert
^L  find next   ^KL to line No.  ^K/ filter ^^ redo            ^KD save
test.dat
```

joe's screen splits to show the basic help commands. Anytime that you see a ^, you should press (CTRL). Notice that commands such as those for moving forward or backward a screen at a time are provided as well as commands for moving to the start or end of the file. Searching commands, blocking commands (for copying, cutting, and pasting), deletion commands, and file commands are all provided on this one screen.

If you want to turn the help screen off again, just look at the screen for instructions on how to do so. The top line says to press (CTRL)-**K H** again to turn help off.

In summary, *joe* is an easy-to-use editor that behaves similar to most word processors. *joe* provides numerous navigation tools on the screen to allow even new users to become productive with the editor with a minimal amount of time and practice.

pico

pico is very similar in its design and use to *joe*. The screen provides most of the navigation tools that you need to get your work done. *pico* allows the cursor keys to move the cursor around within the editor. The (BACKSPACE) key acts as you expect. Just as with *vi* and *joe*, you should specify a filename after the *pico* command. Let's start *pico*.

```
zard:~$ pico test.dat

UW PICO(tm) 2.5                 File: test.dat


  :

                    [ New file ]
^G Get Help  ^O WriteOut  ^R Read File ^Y Prev Pg  ^K Cut Text  ^C Cur Pos
^X Exit      ^J Justify   ^W Where is  ^V Next Pg  ^U UnCut Text^T To Spell
```

Notice that *pico* provides the name of the file being edited at the top of the screen and the [New file] prompt toward the bottom. When you are using *pico*, you should look toward the bottom of the screen for navigation information.

There are only two important keystrokes that *pico* users should be aware of.

pico Keystroke	What It Does
(CTRL)-G	Gets help on using pico
(CTRL)-X	Exits the pico editor

Just as with *joe*, the control key is represented on the *pico* screen as ^. Let's press (CTRL)-**G** to see what help is available from *pico*. Actually I scrolled through the entire help system to print all of the commands for your viewing:

```
UW PICO(tm) 2.5              File: test.dat

Pico Help Text

Pico is designed to be a simple, easy-to-use text editor with a
layout very similar to the pine mailer.  The status line at the
top of the display shows pico's version, the current file being
edited and whether or not there are outstanding modifications
that have not been saved.  The third line from the bottom is used
to report informational messages and for additional command input.
The bottom two lines list the available editing commands.

Each character typed is automatically inserted into the buffer
at the current cursor position.  Editing commands and cursor
movement (besides arrow keys) are given to pico by typing
special control-key sequences.  A caret, '^', is used to denote
the control key, sometimes marked "CTRL", so the CTRL-q key
combination is written as ^Q.

The following functions are available in pico (where applicable,
corresponding function key commands are in parentheses).

^G (F1)    Display this help text.

^F         move Forward a character.
^B         move Backward a character.
^P         move to the Previous line.
^N         move to the Next line.
^A         move to the beginning of the current line.
^E         move to the End of the current line.
^V (F8)    move forward a page of text.
^Y (F7)    move backward a page of text.

^W (F6)    Search for (where is) text, neglecting case.
^L         Refresh the display.

^D         Delete the character at the cursor position.
^^         Mark cursor position as beginning of selected text.
   Note: Setting mark when already set unselects text.
^K (F9)    Cut selected text (displayed in inverse characters).
   Note: The selected text's boundary on the cursor side ends at the
left edge of the cursor.  So, with selected text to the left of the
cursor, the character under the cursor is not selected.
^U (F10) Uncut (paste) last cut text inserting it at the current cur-
sor position.
^I         Insert a tab at the current cursor position.

^J (F4)    Format (justify) the current paragraph.
   Note: paragraphs delimited by blank lines or indentation.
^T (F12)  To invoke the spelling checker
^C (F11)  Report current cursor position

^R (F5)    Insert an external file at the current cursor position.
^O (F3)    Output the current buffer to a file, saving it.
^X (F2)    Exit pico, saving buffer.

Pine and Pico are trademarks of the University of Washington.
No commercial use of these trademarks may be made without prior
written permission of the University of Washington.

        End of Help.
```

To get out of the help system, I press (CTRL)-**X**.

One more item to look at in *pico* is how do you save files versus quitting the editor without saving. To see how this is done, I am going to type one line into the editor and then press (CTRL)-**X**, which is the onscreen navigation tool for exiting from the editor.

```
UW PICO(tm) 2.5         File: test.dat           Modified

Typed into pico


        :

Save modified buffer (ANSWERING "No" WILL DESTROY CHANGES) ?
                Y Yes
^C Cancel       N No
```

Notice that pressing the exit combination returns a prompt asking whether or not I want to save the changes. Answering **Y** saves my changes to the file and then gets me out of the editor. Answering **N** tells *pico* to ignore my changes to the file and simply quit the editor. The other option is to press the (CTRL)-**C** combination to cancel the attempted save/quit command. It is worthwhile to note the single key-stroke used to save or quit in pico, versus the separate commands needed in editors such as *vi* and *joe*.

emacs

emacs is another editor that is somewhat widespread on UNIX systems. Although *emacs* is not as user friendly as *joe* or *pico*, it is still much easier to use than *vi* and actually the most powerful of the editors that are examined in this section. *emacs* permits mini "programs" to be written within the editor so that it can be extended by the user. The discussion here of *emacs* will be limited to the basics of the editor.

Moving the cursor around on the screen works the same way as the other editors in that you use the arrow keys. Let's take a look at starting up *emacs*:

```
zard:~$ emacs test.dat

 :

-----Emacs: test.dat      (Fundamental)--All----------------------------
(New file)
```

Other than the fact that *emacs* tells me this is a new file, there aren't any informational or navigational items displayed. *emacs* also makes extensive use of the (CTRL) key. C- is the *emacs* version of ^, which in any case, means press the (CTRL) key. Here's an example of pressing what *emacs* calls the C-h keystroke, which displays help (I actually pressed (CTRL)-h):

```
--**-Emacs: test.dat      (Fundamental)--All----------------------------
You have typed C-h, the help character.  Type a Help option:
(Use SPC or DEL to scroll through this text.  Type q to exit the Help com-
mand.)

a  command-apropos.  Give a substring, and see a list of commands
        (functions interactively callable) that contain
        that substring.  See also the apropos  command.
b  describe-bindings.  Display table of all key bindings.
c  describe-key-briefly.  Type a command key sequence;
        it prints the function name that sequence runs.
f  describe-function.  Type a function name and get documentation of it.
C-f Info-goto-emacs-command-node.  Type a function name;
--**-Emacs: *Help*        (Help)--Top----------------------------------
Global Bindings:
key            binding
---            -------
C-@            set-mark-command
C-a            beginning-of-line
C-b            backward-char
C-c            mode-specific-command-prefix
C-d            delete-char
C-e            end-of-line
C-f            forward-char
-----Emacs: *Help*        (Help)--Top----------------------------------
```

As you can see, the *emacs* help system isn't as user-friendly as those of the other editors.

The remainder of this section will look at the common *emacs* commands you will need. In addition to the C- notation, which means (CTRL), *emacs* uses the notation M-, which means press *meta,* or the (ALT) key. Sometimes these keystrokes will be used together, such as C-M-, which means press the (CTRL) and (ALT) keys at the same time.

Saving, Exiting, and Help Commands

emacs Command	What It Does
C-x C-s	Saves the file being edited
C-x C-c	Exits from the editor
C-x C-w	Saves the file being edited but asks for a new name

Cursor Movement Commands

emacs Command	What It Does
C-p	Moves up one line
C-n	Moves down one line
C-f	Moves forward one character
C-b	Moves back one character
C-v	Moves forward one screen
M-v	Moves backward one screen
C-a	Goes to the beginning of the line
C-e	Goes to the end of the line
M->	Moves to the top of the file
M-<	Moves to the bottom of the file

Insertion and Deletion Commands

emacs Command	What It Does
C-c	Inserts a space
C-j	Inserts a new line and indents
DEL	Deletes the previous character
C-d	Deletes the character at the cursor
M-d	Deletes a word
C-k	Deletes a line

Search and Replace Commands

emacs Command	What It Does
C-s	Searches forward
C-r	Searches backward
META	Exits a successful search
C-g	Cancels a search
M-r	Replaces all copies of the first string with the second string, each ending with the meta key
M-C-r	Asks before performing the replacement

Appendix B: Introduction to X Windows

X Windows is a graphical user environment that has been created for many versions of UNIX. If you are familiar with Microsoft Windows, you should have little trouble learning and using X Windows. Just as there are several flavors of UNIX, there are several vendor versions of X Windows available: Sun Microsystems has OpenWindows, Hewlett-Packard has OpenLook, and Next has NextStep. This section provides a brief overview of the basic X Windows environment.

Starting X Windows

X Windows is usually started in one of two different ways. Some versions of X Windows may start as you login to your UNIX computer. If your computer is capable of running X Windows and leaves you at the command prompt when you login, you will have to type in a command to start X Windows. Here's an example of starting X Windows on my computer.

```
zard:~$ startx
```

After a few seconds, I see the inital X Windows screen.

Figure B-1
X-Windows Screen

Using the Mouse with X Windows

Most mice that are used on UNIX systems have three buttons. The default assignments of the buttons depend upon the version of X Windows being used. The version of X Windows that I use sets the left mouse button up for displaying menus, the middle mouse button for window controls, and the right mouse button for adjusting the environment. The OpenWindows version uses the left mouse button for selection (of text or objects onscreen), the middle mouse button for environment adjustment, and the right mouse button for menu display.

You have to be cautious about double-clicking the mouse in X Windows. If you are a Microsoft Windows user, this particular aspect of X Windows will cause you more irritation than anything else since double-clicking will not always do what you expect. Also be aware that on most two-button mice, you can simulate the third button on a three-button mouse by pressing both mouse buttons at the same time.

Menus in X Windows

As in most GUIs, X Windows provides the majority of its functionality to the user through menus. To open the main menu on my version of X Windows, I hold down the left mouse button while pointing at a blank spot on the background of the screen. (Figure B-2).

Any time that you see a small arrow, either pointing right or pointing down, there is a submenu under that menu item. Figure B-3 is an example of what comes up when I slide down to the Shells option on my main menu.

Figure B-2
X-Windows Menus

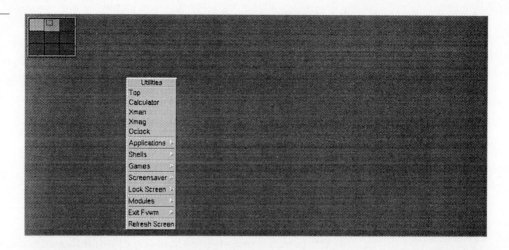

Figure B-3
X-Windows Submenu

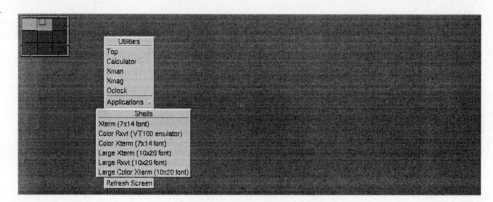

By sliding over to the Xterm option and letting go of the left mouse button, I have indicated to X Windows that I want it to start the Xterm program. The Xterm program is simply a UNIX shell in a window from which I can type UNIX commands.

Figure B-4
**Xterm
Window**

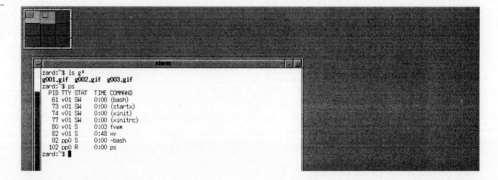

Exiting X Windows

Exiting the X Windows system is easy. You simply need to display the main menu by clicking the left mouse button and then choose *Exit*. In the submenu that appears, select the *Yes, Really Quit* response, and X Windows shuts down and will either automatically log you out of the system or drop you back to a UNIX command prompt. What happens depends upon your particular system. Here's an example of the *Exit* menu on my system.

Figure B-5
Exit X Windows menu

X Windows Basics

X Windows windows are very similar to those in Microsoft Windows. All windows can be moved, resized, minimized, maximized, and closed. You can access the control menu by moving the mouse pointer to the dash symbol in the upper left-hand corner of a window and then clicking the left mouse button. Here's an example of the pull-down menu that you will see.

Figure B-6
**Window
Control Menu**

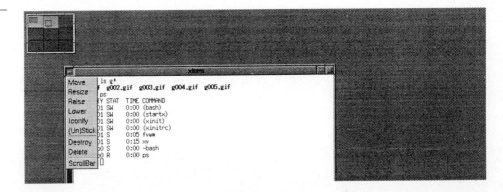

The little square in the upper right-hand corner will shrink the open window down to an icon on the desktop, whereas the large square will maximize the window to fill the entire screen.

Using the Desktop

Many X Windows versions allow you to work with a screen area larger than what can physically be viewed on the screen. This is known as a virtual desktop. The desktop is your workspace where all of your applications will be displayed and can be minimized or maximized. Take a look at the following screen, and notice the small rectangular region up in the left corner.

Figure B-7
X Windows Desktop

You can work with a desktop nine times the size of the monitor. To move to a new region, simply click the left mouse button on the area that you want to work with. This allows you to work with multiple applications simultaneously and spread them out so that they are easy to access and use.

You also have other mouse controls that affect the desktop under X Windows. You can press the right mouse button to see all the windows that are open. You can move to any window simply by pressing the right mouse button and then pointing at the window you want to go to. When you release the mouse, you will be at that window.

Pressing the middle button (or pressing both left and right buttons simultaneously on a two-button mouse) displays a list of Windows controls similar to what you see when you click the control menu on a window. Here's an example.

Figure B-8
Windows Controls

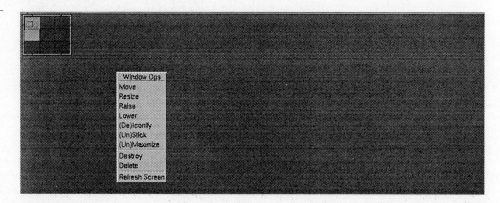

Basic X Windows Applications

X Windows provides a number of basic applications. Here is a partial list of those applications.

- Xterm is a text-based command-line interpreter.
- xedit is an interactive text editor.

Figure B-9
xedit

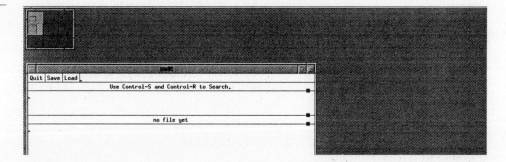

- Xfilemanager is a graphical file management program.
- OClock is real-time display of the current time and date with a stopwatch feature.
- Calculator is a scientific calculator.

Figure B-10
Calculator

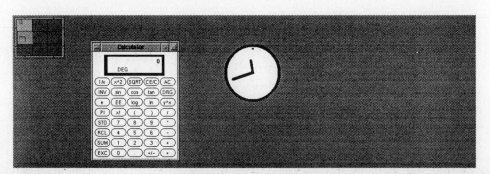

■ xpaint is a drawing application.

Figure B-11
xpaint

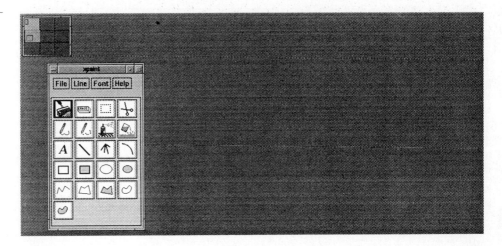

Summary

This appendix introduced you to some of the basic concepts of X Windows. You should ask your instructor or computer center about the version of X Windows your school has available. You should then refer to a book on working with that particular version of X Windows to get the maximum use from your graphical UNIX workstations.

Appendix C: Commands Summary

Name	Purpose	Syntax	Options	Section
&	Places a process in the background	*command* &		4-2
at	Specifies the time when a command should be performed	at *time command*		4-4
bc	Basic calculator	bc		4-6
bg	Places a process in the background	bg		4-2
cal	Displays a calendar	cal cal *month year* cal *year*		4-6
cat	Displays the contents of a file	cat *filename*		2-4
cc	Compiles C programs	cc *options progname*	–o Specifies the name of the executable	4-1
cd	Changes directory	cd *directoryname*		2-2
chmod	Changes the permission (rwx) of a file or directory	chmod *value file/dirname*		2-7

Name	Purpose	Syntax	Options	Section
clear	Clears the screen	clear		4-6
compress	Compresses a file	compress *filename*		4-5
cp	Copies files	cp *options source destination*	-i Confirms copy operation	2-5
cron	Permits the automatic scheduling and running of processes	Edit the crontab file		4-4
date	Displays the current system date and time	date		4-4
diff	Displays any differences between two files	diff *filename1 filename2*		4-6
echo	Displays messages on the screen	echo "*message*"		4-6
elm	Menu driven e-mail system	elm elm *username* elm *username@hostname*		3-2
emacs	Text editor	emacs *filename*		App. A
exit	Logs a user out of the computer system	exit		2-1
f77	Compiles Fortran 77 programs	f77 *options progname*	-o Specifies the name of the executable	4-1
fg	Brings a process from the background to the foreground	fg *jobnumber*		4-2
find	Locates files on the computer	find *directorytostart option*	-exec *command* Specifies a command to be perfomed on the files that were found -mtime Specifies modification time -name Specifies the name of the files to look for -print Displays the names of the files that were found -user Specifies the user who owns the files	4-6
finger	Displays information on users that are logged on to the system	finger finger *username* finger *username@hostname*		3-1
ftp	Used to transfer files over the network	ftp ftp *hostname*		3-3
gopher	Used to access the gopher information source	gopher		3-4
grep	Searches files for a specified phrase	grep "*phrase*" *filelist*		4-6

Name	Purpose	Syntax	Options	Section
gzip	Compresses and uncompresses files	gzip *option gzipfilename*	-d Uncompresses the file	4-5
head	Displays the first ten lines of a file	head *filename*		2-4
jobs	Lists the processes that you have running in the background	jobs		4-2
joe	Text editor	joe *filename*		App. A
kill	Stops a process that you have running	kill *option processnumber*	-9 Specifies the process should be terminated immediately	4-2
logout	Logs a user out of the computer system	logout		2-1
lpq	Checks the printer queue status	lpq *options*	-Pname Specifies a particular printer	2-6
lpr	Prints files	lpr *options filename*	-Pname Specifies a particular printer #value Specifies the number of copies to print	2-6
lprm	Removes a job from the printer queue	lprm *options jobnumber*	-Pname Specifies a particular printer	2-6
ls	Displays the contents of a directory	ls *options file/dirname*	-l Indicates a long listing -a Displays all files -F Marks directories and executables	2-2
lynx	Text-based Web browser	lynx		3-4
mail	The basic UNIX e-mail system	mail *username* mail *username@hostname*		3-2
man	The UNIX help system	man *command*		2-9
mesg	Turns messaging off	mesg n mesg y		4-6
mkdir	Makes directory	mkdir *directoryname*		2-2
more	Displays the contents of a file or piped output one screen at a time	more *filename* *processoutput* | more		2-4
mv	Renames or moves files	mv *filename*		2-5
nice	Changes the priority of a process	nice *level processnumber*		4-3
nn	Used to read UseNet News	nn		3-4
nslookup	Displays the IP address or hostname for a computer	nslookup *hostname* nslookup *IPaddress*		3-1
passwd	Allows user to change password	passwd		2-1
pico	Text editor	pico *filename*		App. A

Name	Purpose	Syntax	Options	Section
ping	Checks if a computer is accessible from the network	ping *hostname*		3-1
ps	Shows processes that you have running	ps		4-2
pwd	Prints working directory	pwd		2-2
rm	Removes files	rm *filename*		2-5
rmdir	Remove sdirectory	rmdir *directoryname*		2-2
sort	Sorts the contents of a file	sort *filename option*	-o *filename* Specifies that the sorted contents should be written to another file	4-6
tail	Displays the last ten lines of a file	tail *filename*		2-4
talk	Split-screen communication between two users	talk *username* talk *username@hostname*		3-1
tar	Creates an archive of files	tar *option tarfilename*	-c Creates the tar file -f Specifies the filename -t Tests the tar file -v Verbose listing -x Extracts files from the tar file	4-5
telnet	Used to login to a computer on the network	telnet telnet *hostname*		3-3
uncompress	Uncompresses a compressed file	uncompress *filename*		4-5
uptime	Shows how long the computer system has been operational and what the load average is	uptime		4-3
vi	Text editor	vi *filename*		App. A
w	Displays the users that are logged on to the system and what each user is doing	w		3-1
who	Displays the users that are logged on to the system	who		3-1
whoami	Displays information concerning how you are logged on to the system	whoami who am i		3-1
whois	Displays any information on a user from the InterNIC database	whois *username* whois *username@hostname*		3-1
write	Writes a message to a particular user's screen	write *username message*		4-6

Index